This book belongs to

CHEF JUNIOR

yum!

CHEF JUNIOR

100 Super Delicious Recipes by Kids for Kids!

WILL BARTLETT · KATIE DESSINGER

PAUL KIMBALL · ABIGAIL LANGFORD

ANTHONY SPEARS

STERLING EPICURE
New York

STERLING EPICURE
New York

An Imprint of Sterling Publishing Co., Inc.
1166 Avenue of the Americas
New York, NY 10036

ISBN 978-1-4549-3361-8

Distributed in Canada by Sterling Publishing Co., Inc.
c/o Canadian Manda Group, 664 Annette Street
Toronto Canada M6S 2C8, Ontario,
Distributed in the United Kingdom by GMC Distribution Services
Castle Place, 166 High Street, Lewes, East Sussex BN7 1XU, England
Distributed in Australia by NewSouth Books
University of New South Wales, Sydney, NSW 2052, Australia

For information about custom editions, special sales, and premium and corporate purchases,
please contact Sterling Special Sales at 800-805-5489 or specialsales@sterlingpublishing.com.

Manufactured in Malaysia

2 4 6 8 10 9 7 5 3 1

sterlingpublishing.com

Cover design by Jo Obarowski
Interior design by Shannon Nicole Plunkett

Illustrations by Ku_suriuri/Shutterstock.com and ivo_13/Getty Images

Contents

About the Authors >>> 6

Real Food >>> 10

How to Use the Equipment in this Book >>> 13

Using Knives Safely >>> 17

How to Substitute Ingredients to Make Recipes Allergy-Friendly >>> 20

THE RECIPES

Breakfast >>> 25

Lunch >>> 49

Dinner >>> 95

Snacks >>> 137

Dessert >>> 171

Drinks >>> 191

Meal Planning Like a Pro >>> 200

Metric Conversion Charts >>> 202

Index >>> 203

About THE AUTHORS

WILL BARTLETT

I'm thirteen and still live in California, where I was born. In 2017, I traveled the world with my family, tasting and trying all kinds of weird food, from bean donuts (found in a small store in the winding streets of Japan) to the best steak I've ever had (also found in Japan in a restaurant in Kyoto). Our travels allowed me to get to know a little more about people around the world and how they eat. For example, after a forty-five-mile bike ride through tiny villages and green rice paddies, we dined in our guide's traditional Balinese home. We ate a village chicken killed that morning, rice from their fields, and vegetables from the garden next to their family temple. In the Philippines, I ate the sweetest mango I ever tasted.

Food makes people unique. I remember certain people because of the food they shared, and the love they spread.

I think we should all be able to enjoy the excitement of baking a loaf of bread or cooking a meal from scratch. I love eating, but everything tastes better when you have made it yourself.

One of my other passions is basketball. I love playing the sport, and even more, I love the massive appetite you get after playing it. One of my favorite drinks is a smoothie. I drink one almost every day, no matter the weather. I also like bacon and avocado. I bet you guys are all groaning right now thinking, "Typical Californian, loves avocado." I can't lie, that's true.

PAUL KIMBALL

I'm fifteen and live in the rather cold state of Michigan with my three siblings. I enjoy mastering Rubik's™ cubes and dancing hip-hop.

When I was younger, it felt like cooking was a "girl thing." For example, after my mom was born, my Polish grandpa, Dzia Dzia, was alone at home. He put a whole pound of ground beef into a pan and ate it for dinner. Even though many guys can't cook, cooking really is for everyone. Your age and gender don't matter. In fact, when I was two, I was in the kitchen using a butter knife.

The famous chef Bobby Flay once said, "I just wanted to cook, period." Simple—his enthusiasm is flat-out why I want to cook. I want to share my knowledge about cooking so that other people can learn to cook.

One of the reasons my mom taught me to cook is so I won't have to eat frozen pizzas and canned soup when I go to college. I totally agree, because who wants to eat processed food for four years? Sometimes I imagine cooking my favorite dish, cheeseburger soup, for my roommates. Picturing all of them digging in highlights an important aspect of cooking: making food that other people like. Cooking food is "just okay" if you're cooking for yourself, but when you cook for other people, their approval is motivating. It is my hope that you make the recipes in this cookbook for friends and relatives, because bringing people together for a delicious meal is what cooking is all about. It starts with you just wanting to cook, period.

ABIGAIL LANGFORD

I'm fifteen, and I live in Kelowna, Canada.

For me, food is full of memories. I mean, think about it. Think of your top five favorite memories. I'll bet one of them revolves around food. My first food memory goes back to when I was four. I was having dinner with my family—salad, meat, and corn on the cob, a very dinner-like meal. And I remember taking a giant blob of butter from the butter dish and plopping it onto my plate, right next to my corn. I then proceeded to roll the warm corn in the butter, giving it a sort of glaze. It looked sooo good. I took a massive bite into the corn cob, crunching too far into the middle. I heard a *crrraaaccckkk*, and then my tooth popped out of my mouth. That's still one of my favorite memories—ten years later.

As a small child, cooking mesmerized me. We had a little toy kitchen in the playroom. There were all sorts of utensils, pots, pans, different kinds of food, and even a microwave and a realistic sink. One of the things I loved most about that toy kitchen was a little flipper made of metal. I thought it was so cute and just perfectly my size. So one day, while my mom was making pancakes, I asked if I could help her flip them with my toy flipper. She examined it for dangerous parts and, when she found nothing, let me get a chair from the table and bring it up to the stove to help with the flipping.

I can only hope that this book will inspire you to love food as much as I do.

ANTHONY SPEARS

I'm thirteen years old and live in Florida with my parents and five siblings. I love reading, nature, playing with my siblings, and hanging out with my best friends, Paul and Caden. I've hung out in the kitchen with my parents as long as I can remember. My favorite food is probably poutine (fries with cheese curds and gravy), which I first got to try when visiting friends in Canada. Cooking is one of those things that I feel is really a part of me.

I've always been fascinated to learn where food comes from, what makes food taste great, and what makes food good for you. My family always had a garden, and I always helped out pulling weeds, watering plants, picking vegetables, and even digging up sweet potatoes. I was amazed at how much time and patience went into growing the vegetables for even one meal, and I always understood that quality food involves hard work and dedication. It also really stuck with me that food seemed to taste better when it was fresh and in season and I had a hand in growing it.

When I was six years old, I didn't think that I liked seafood very much, but then, one day on vacation, my dad took me fishing. After a long day of waiting, I caught a small white fish. My dad taught me how to clean, season, and cook it (I recommend butter, garlic, and lemon). To my surprise, I found that I really liked the taste. I also felt a sense of pride for having worked so hard to make that meal. From that day on, I came to realize just how empowering it feels to be able to prepare an entire meal completely from scratch, especially when you get to source the food yourself.

My hope with this cookbook is that it will awaken your passion for delicious, real food and give you the tools to cook it in your own kitchen for your own family.

KATIE DESSINGER

I'm twelve, and I live by the turquoise-blue waves of the Florida coast. The sun is so bright here that you can grow vegetables almost all year-round if you have good soil. If we had a chance to sit down and talk, we could swap stories of adventures and experiments and probably make believe we're Narnian explorers, which eventually would lead us to a great feast. And what would we eat? We'd start by baking bread. Every feast needs bread! My family's diet is gluten-free, so our feast would include fabulous gluten-free bread with homemade strawberry jam. You'll find recipes for both in this book.

I love to take on new challenges on my own and learn new skills. When I was three, I helped my mom make pasta from scratch. She has dozens of photos of me rolling dough and making a mess with my chubby cheeks smiling as big as can be. I also remember trying to catch fish in a stream when I was six years old. I brought home one tiny minnow in my net and begged my mom to cook it for lunch. I was so proud. And I'm telling you, it was the tastiest fish I'd ever eaten. Then, when I was seven, I found persimmons and wild mint on our property and ran home each time to announce my discovery. We ate the persimmons and made mint tea; it was so much fun. Discovering, testing, and experimenting are all part of the food memories I will treasure forever.

I want you to have your own food memories, too. Even if you're not used to trying new things, pick one recipe that sounds yummy from the book and explore something new. If you're not sure that cooking is your thing, I get it. It looks hard. It sounds hard. And sometimes it is. But it doesn't have to be, especially if you love tasting new flavors and trying new foods.

REAL FOOD

BY ANTHONY

Any great chef will tell you that a meal is only as good as its ingredients. Quality food can make a meal taste so much better, and, in general, these foods are healthier for us as well. The foods we eat have changed a lot since our grandparents and great-grandparents were kids. In fact, what we call organic food these days was the only type of food they ate less than a hundred years ago. There was no need to certify or classify it as organic or natural because everything already was. You're probably wondering why any of this is important. The reason is that healthy organic food is better for you, the animals, the environment, and pretty much the entire world.

WHAT IS REAL FOOD?

An easy rule of thumb is that if something doesn't have ingredients, but IS an ingredient (one thing), it is generally healthier for you. For example, a piece of fruit and a cookie may have the same amount of sugar in them, but the fruit came directly from nature and only has one ingredient. The cookie could have up to 40 ingredients (or even more!) and won't provide your body with the same good stuff—fiber, water content, or vitamins—that the fruit will.

As you start buying food and creating meals, you'll find a lot of different options to choose from, and many foods are labeled with different terms. The best-tasting foods and the best ones for you

start with real whole foods that have not been sprayed with lots of pesticides and have not been genetically modified or, in the case of animals, that have been fed and raised properly. Finding these foods can be tricky! You'll see all kinds of terms, like *natural*, *organic*, *grass-fed*, *pasture raised*, *vegan*, and others and may wonder what they all mean. I'm going to help you out with that.

BUYING PRODUCE

The produce aisle in any store is a great place to start. Most experts agree that we need to eat vegetables to be healthy and that most of us are not eating enough of them. Less than a century ago, people consumed an average of 250 types of plants each year, and now most of us only consume the same 10 to 20 over and over. When you're thinking about planning meals or snacks, start with veggies and add protein and healthy fats from there. These foods have things like fiber, micronutrients, and other compounds that make our guts and whole bodies healthier.

In the produce aisle, you'll have the option of buying either organic or conventional fruits and vegetables.

Now, let's be real for a second.

Organic food is usually more expensive, so you may want to prioritize which organic foods you buy. The Dirty Dozen™ list shows the foods most

You can tell if a food is organic or not by looking at the number on the price look-up (PLU) sticker. Vegetables are labeled with PLU stickers so that the store can check them out even if they don't also have a price sticker. For instance, if a banana doesn't have a barcode or sticker, the checkout cashier will know that the code is 4011 and can type it in. An organic banana has a 9 in front of that number, so its PLU would be 94011 instead. So, if you're trying to figure out if something is organic or not, check to see if its PLU number starts with a 9!

likely to be contaminated with large amounts of pesticides, so you'll want to buy only organic foods on this list. The Clean Fifteen™ list shows the ones most likely to be safe, even if they are not organic. These lists can change every year, so look them up on the Internet to be sure.

THE DIRTY DOZEN—Buy Organic Only

Strawberries	Apples	Pears
Spinach	Grapes	Tomatoes
Kale	Peaches	Celery
Nectarines	Cherries	Potatoes

THE CLEAN FIFTEEN
—No Need to Buy Organic

Avocados	Papayas	Cauliflower
Sweet corn	Eggplants	Cantaloupes
Pineapples	Asparagus	Broccoli
Frozen sweet peas	Kiwis	Mushrooms
	Cabbages	Honeydew melons
Onions		

BUYING MEAT, DAIRY, AND EGGS

Things get a little trickier when it comes to meat and dairy. Now, in addition to the organic label, you'll see other labels as well. You'll find terms like *natural*, *pasture raised*, *grass-fed*, and many others.

Often, the best option is to buy from a local farmer who can tell you how the animals were raised and what they were fed. Below, you'll find out what grocery store labels really mean.

GROCERY STORE LABELS FOR MEAT AND DAIRY

Organic—Look for this label! On meats and dairy, this means that the cows are not given antibiotics or growth hormones, are raised outdoors, and are fed organic food. If eggs are labeled organic, then hens are fed organic grass and are free range. These are all good things!

Natural—This term is used a lot on many food labels, but it doesn't necessarily mean anything on its own, so if you see it, ignore it.

Grass-fed—Cows like grass and should eat grass. This label means that the cows have plenty of room to graze and access to grass most of the year except in the winter, when alfalfa or other plant substitutes are used.

Pasture raised—This term usually appears on egg cartons and means that the hens that laid those eggs are raised in open grassy pastures and eat insects and worms.

Cage-free—This term is used for both poultry and eggs. This means that the chickens are not raised in cages, but it does not mean they necessarily have access to outdoor spaces. Unlike conventional egg farming, cage-free in most cases means the hens have enough room to dust bath, forage, perch, and other conditions chickens have in the wild.

Free-range—Free-range means the animal the product came from has plenty of room to roam around in open grassy fields.

BUYING FISH AND SEAFOOD

When it comes to seafood, there are a few factors to consider. Some seafood is safe to eat, but not if it's caught or farmed in a way that isn't safe for the planet, or if it contains high mercury levels. As more and more plastic pollution builds up in the ocean, fish are becoming contaminated with plastic, too.

When you search for fish and seafood, you'll see terms like *wild caught* or, more rarely, *organic*. There's a big range of options with a big range in price and quality. Most people don't live near an ocean or a large body of water, where fishing is an option, but if you do, look for a place to fish (with a permit or license if needed) and ask your local Fish and Wildlife Department if the fish are safe to eat. If you're buying fish, try to stick with ones that are sustainable and considered safe. Smaller fish are usually more sustainable and contain less mercury and other heavy metals.

THE TOP FIVE FISH TO TRY

Canned salmon (with bones) wild caught from Alaska

Canned wild caught sardines

Salmon, wild caught from Alaska (fresh or frozen)

Freshwater Coho salmon (from the US, farmed in tank systems)

Atlantic mackerel

THE TOP FISH TO AVOID

Bluefin tuna

Catfish

Mahi mahi

Orange roughy

Atlantic Halibut (look for Pacific Halinut instead)

Chilean sea bass

WHERE TO SHOP

Most of us are familiar with shopping at a grocery store, but once you start to learn about making your own food, you'll find there are some really creative ways to find healthy food, from farmers markets and local markets to CSAs and cow shares. You can even grow your own.

Why Buy Local?

Local food is fresher and tastes better than food that has been trucked or flown in from thousands of miles away. Those thousands of miles lead to a big carbon footprint for a few fruits or vegetables. And local food tastes better, too. Buying food at local stores and markets also helps support your local economy, and you get to meet some of the people that grow or raise your food.

Growing Your Own Food

Growing your own food is really fun, and it's the best way to get the freshest food and save some money, too. Every year my mom and I plant a garden in our backyard. Some of our favorite things to grow are sweet potatoes, strawberries, romaine lettuce, and tomatoes. My grandpa and I even have a beehive in his backyard. But no matter where you live—even in a small house or apartment with no yard—you can grow sprouts or micro greens on your kitchen counter. Look online for some easy tutorials about how to do this.

How to Use the Equipment in This Book

By Abigail

Preparing food is a skill, and before you start to cook, you'll need to know how to handle the equipment you will be using. Of course, always cook with an adult at your side, and before you even attempt to handle any of the essential kitchen tools and appliances listed below, have them demonstrate how they work. Safety comes first, especially in the kitchen. Let's jump in!

FOOD PROCESSOR

The powerful food processor is great for chopping any vegetable into small or very small pieces super quickly with a very sharp rotating blade. It can also purée food into mushy things, like dips and spreads, or even liquefy foods to make soups and dressings. In this book, you'll even use the processor to make things like pastry dough and date balls. The food processor also comes with shredding and slicing attachments to shred things (like cheese or carrots) or slice things (like cheese or cucumbers). You'll use the feed tube and plunger to "feed" and push the vegetable down to the whirling blade of the attachment.

Let's get into using the machine safely. When a recipe calls for a food processor, place it on the counter, but **do not plug it into an electrical socket**. You will need to carefully lock the large plastic container onto the base of the machine and carefully fit the blade into the container or arrange the shredding or slicing attachments into the base of the bowl. Next, get the vegetables ready. You may need to cut them up into a couple of large chunks so that they will fit in the food processor to be chopped, or cut them into long pieces so that they can be passed through a feed tube, if you are using it to slice or shred.

The reason we prep food before plugging in the processor is simply because mistakes can happen. If the machine is plugged in while you are putting the vegetables into the container you can accidentally bump a button and turn the machine on. So, in order to be extra safe, always leave it unplugged until you are ready to turn it on. It is very important that you use the food processor with adult supervision. Machines vary, and you should have an adult show you how to set yours up and how it works.

STOVETOP

I have a little secret that I need to get off my chest: I'm afraid of stoves. Once, when I was babysitting my siblings (my parents were out of the house), I had to make lunch. I thought I could make deep-fried bacon-wrapped dates. Now, you may not know this (and neither did I), but deep-frying is very dangerous, and kids aren't supposed to try it. To make a very long story short, I thought the oil would bubble and come to a boil, but instead it smoked. Then I tried to cool down the mess with water . . . another big mistake. The pot of hot oil and water exploded! Why am I telling you this? Well, because of my crazy experience, I've learned a lot about using the stove safely, and I really want to teach you everything I've learned so that you don't make the same mistakes.

The first and most important rule: **Kids should never try to deep-fry anything.** Ever. Even boiling water can also be dangerous! Imagine if a big pot of boiling water fell over! We have a few pasta recipes in this book that require you to boil the noodles in a pot of boiling water. Make sure that an adult is with you while the water boils, and have them drain the pasta for you.

Next, **always have a fire extinguisher nearby**. Ask an adult where a fire extinguisher is in your house, and have them show you how to use it.

Here's another tip. **When cooking anything on the stovetop, always keep the pan handle turned away from the front of the stove.** Anyone could walk by without paying attention and accidentally knock the handle, and that can cause the hot pan and its contents to fall off the stove, causing great injury.

Next, and this is important: **NEVER leave something on the stove and walk away.** When you are an adult and feel totally assured, that may be another story, but a young chef should never leave something cooking on the stove unattended for even a minute.

Another rule? Turn the stove fan on and keep it on the whole time you're cooking. You don't want smoke filling up the kitchen.

And remember, even a moderately hot burner, pot, or pan can burn your fingers in seconds. Never flip food with your fingers, and don't touch hot burners or pots.

OVEN

Baking and roasting something in the oven requires intense heat, so you really need to pay attention to what you are doing. Only turn on the oven when you are with an adult who is supervising you and when you aren't distracted. All recipes will tell you the exact temperature that is needed, so all you need to do is to turn the oven on to the correct temperature and wait for it to heat up to that temperature. Be sure to use the correct size baking pan or dish, so that the contents, particularly grease, don't drip into the bottom of the hot oven.

To protect your hands from getting burned, always wear oven mitts whenever you are putting something in or taking something out of a hot oven, and set a timer to keep the food from overcooking and burning. A good rule is to never leave the kitchen while you are using the oven. And, of course, turn off the oven immediately once you are finished using it. To be extra safe, always double-check to make sure the oven is off before you leave the kitchen.

BLENDER

A blender, with its sharp blades, can be a little freaky. Here are a couple rules to follow: First, keep it unplugged until you are ready to turn it on. Putting the lid on correctly is important, too. If you don't, and the blender gets turned on, you'll have a huge mess (and trust me, it isn't fun to clean up). Finally, when you turn on the blender, start from the lowest number setting and work your way up to the highest number setting. If you don't, it can ruin the blender (plus make a scary noise). Also, it's a good idea to keep your hand on the lid of the blender most of the time. That way, if anything happens, you are right there to fix it.

IMMERSION BLENDER

An immersion blender is a little more dangerous than a regular blender because the blades are actually exposed. So, the most important thing to remember is to keep the blades pointed away from your fingers at all times! You'll also want to wait until the last second to plug it in (the same way you'd operate a blender or food processor), and make sure to turn it on to the lowest setting first, before increasing the speed. Finally, remember to unplug the immersion blender the minute you've stopped using it, so that no accidents happen.

GRATER

The two basic handheld graters are box graters and flat graters. Box graters stand upright with a handle on the top and have four sides, each of which has different shapes and sizes of holes for grating. Flat graters have a handle and usually just one shape and size of hole. Both graters are easy to use. Ideally, you'll want to work over a large cutting board to catch everything you are grating or shredding. Let's say you have a carrot that needs grating. You want to take the fatter end of the carrot in your hand so that the narrowest part is pointing toward the grater. Now, start rubbing it up and down over the grating holes so that it makes a cutting noise. You should also be able to see small pieces of carrot falling onto the board. When you have only a little bit of the carrot left, just pinch it with your fingertips, to protect your fingers.

Why do I say to protect your fingers? While a grater might not seem very sharp, you can easily skin your finger on the sharp holes on the outside of the grater if you're not paying attention.

PEELER

A peeler is a bit sharper than a grater, but overall it's pretty safe as long as you keep the sharp blade away from your fingers. If you're peeling a carrot, for example, hold the peeler in your dominant hand (the one you write with), because that hand is almost always the strongest. Grab the carrot with your other hand and hold it near the large, fat end. Now, starting from the top of the carrot near the hand that is holding it, place the peeler blade on the surface of the carrot and swipe downward, toward the thinner point of the carrot. Then rotate the carrot and repeat. Do this until all the peel has been removed.

MEASURING CUPS AND SPOONS FOR MEASURING DRY INGREDIENTS

You probably already know that there are two sets of tools for measuring dry ingredients—measuring cups and measuring spoons. Measuring cups come in "nests" of different-size cups that fit inside of one another; measuring spoons are different-size spoons that fit inside of one another, and they often are held together on a ring. The handles on both the cups and spoons have markings that tell you how much the cup or spoon holds.

Measuring cups come in these sizes: ¼ cup; ⅓ cup; ½ cup; ¾ cup; ⅔ cup; and 1 cup.

To measure dry ingredients in the cup measures, take a large spoon and add the ingredient to the cup until the whole measure is full. In the case of flour, add more than enough to fill the cup measure, then, with a flat butter knife, swipe the top of the cup to remove the excess. This will give you an exact measurement.

To measure with spoons, simply dip the spoon into the dry ingredient, and then use a flat butter knife to swipe the excess from the top of the spoon.

GLASS MEASURING CUP FOR MEASURING LIQUID INGREDIENTS

Whenever you need to measure a liquid ingredient, like water, milk, cream, or broth, use a glass measuring cup. A small, 2-cup measuring cup can measure up to 2 cups of liquid; a large 1-quart measuring cup can measure up to 4 cups of liquid. These liquid measuring cups have a handle, and the sides of the cup have measuring lines to indicate ¼ cup, ½ cup, ¾ cup, 1 cup, 1¼ cups, 1½ cups, 1¾ cups, 2 cups, and so on.

To measure a liquid ingredient, place the cup on the counter, pour the liquid into the cup, and stop pouring when the liquid reaches the desired line on the side of the cup. It is best to look at the side of the cup at eye level, so you'll get an accurate measurement. Have an adult show you how to do this properly.

GARLIC PRESS

Although there are many different kinds of garlic presses, most have two handles, a flat piece of metal between the handles, and a small bucket with tiny holes in the bottom. To press the garlic, open the handles wide apart, put a peeled garlic clove into the bucket, place the flat piece of metal over the garlic, and then press the handles together. The pressure will push the garlic through the holes, crushing it into a pasty consistency.

DEHYDRATOR

Dehydrators are handy appliances that remove moisture from food. We use them in this book to make delicious snacks. The main things to remember when using a dehydrator are: keep the lid on, use the right temperatures for the various things you are dehydrating, and read the manual. Oh, and of course, make sure to take the food out on time!

ICE POP MOLD AND STICKS

An ice pop mold can either be a sheet with little (or big) cups in the middle to hold the liquid or little containers with lids that do the same thing. To use them, simply add the liquid mixture that you made with a recipe (we have lots of ice pop recipes in this book!) into the mold or container, put the lid on, and then place it in the freezer—usually overnight is best. When you are ready to unmold your ice pops, take your mold or container to your kitchen sink, put it under warm running water for 5–10 seconds, grab the handle, and the ice pops should slide right out!

USING KNIVES SAFELY

By Paul

Knife skills could quite possibly be the most important thing you need to learn about cooking. You'll use them in just about every recipe you make, from cutting a banana with a butter knife to chopping up potatoes with a chef's knife. Just remember, other than butter knives, all knives must be sharp, because dull ones can slip on foods and cause cuts. Now let's get cutting!

HOW TO HOLD THE KNIFE

First, you have to learn how to hold the knife safely. Grip the knife (not the blade) with your dominant hand (the one you write with), with your palm resting on top of the handle. Wrap all of your fingers and thumb around the handle, shifting your hand closer to the knife blade for more power and control. Make sure your pointer finger isn't on top of the blade, even if you think it gives you more power or control.

Second, you need to move the knife correctly. You should always keep the tip of your knife on the cutting board, and always look at what you are cutting. Whenever you look up, put the knife down, and whenever you are clearing food from your cutting board, put the knife down.

And finally, to be safe, you must learn how to properly hold the food you are cutting.

Basically, there are three ways to hold the food, and they will be used in different situations. As you read through this section, try practicing each of these holds without a knife on a cucumber or onion, or any other food that happens to be lying around. It will help you to know each hold well before you start to use a real knife.

Straight Up-and-Down Hold

This hold is good for longer things, like carrots and cucumbers. Keep the hand that is holding the food as far away from the knife as possible, while still having a good grip on the food. Make sure to keep your fingertips pointed straight down, with the side of your fingers facing the side of the blade of your knife. Keep your thumb straight, directly across the food from your pointer finger:

This keeps your thumb safe from the blade of the knife as you cut the food. If your thumb (or any other fingers) are pointing toward the knife, or your fingers are lying down flat on the food, then there is a great chance that you will cut them.

Fingertip Grip

When the food gets too close to your fingertips, you'll need to change your grip and hold the food with the tips of your fingers. Your knuckles will be facing the side of the knife blade and your thumb will be tucked behind your fingers so that it stays safe. Bend your fingers a little bit. As you are cutting, make sure you don't let the sharp part of the knife go above your curved knuckles. If you keep it below, the side of the blade of your knife can rub against your knuckles but not cut you.

Over the Knife

When you get to the end of a cucumber, carrot, or even an onion, if your hand is big enough, you can put the top of the blade of the knife against your palm and hold the food with your fingers around the knife, with the sharp part against the food. You can even put pressure on the knife with your palm when you cut, to give you more strength.

CHOOSING YOUR KNIFE

It's important to choose the right knife for the job. Make sure your knife is sharp! Here's a quick overview.

Paring knife: Use this little knife for softer and smaller foods (strawberries, pears, mushrooms, etc.).

Medium utility knife: Use this medium-size knife to cut slightly bigger foods that are not too huge and not too hard and may need more precision (apples, cucumbers, zucchini, etc.).

Chef's knife: Use this big knife to cut almost anything else (carrots, potatoes, onions etc.).

Serrated knife: Use this long knife with a sharp jagged blade to slice through soft items, like bread and tomatoes, using a sawing motion.

HOW TO USE THE KNIFE TO CUT DIFFERENT WAYS

Now that you know how to hold a knife, let's talk about the different ways to cut food. As you practice, remember to keep the tip of your knife down on the cutting board.

The Slice

It is best to use a cucumber to practice the slice, because it is softer than most veggies, making it easier to cut without putting much pressure on the knife. Use the straight-up-and-down hold to keep your hand far from the knife. First, cut off the end of the cucumber. To do this, put the tip of the knife on the cutting board so that when you press down, the end of the cucumber will be cut off. Slowly press the sharp edge of the knife blade down to the cutting board. Throw the end away, or you can compost it.

Try cutting a slice of cucumber just like you cut off the end, keeping the tip of your knife on the cutting board at all times. Try to keep the slices about the same size. When you get to the last part of the cucumber, use the over-the-knife hold on the food to cut the last few slices. The slice method will be used on almost all of the veggies you will ever cut, even if you just use it to cut off the ends.

The Dice

When a recipe calls for you to dice a vegetable, you'll need to cut it all up into little cubes. Depending on the vegetable, there are different ways to do this, but basically you are first cutting the vegetable into flat pieces, then cutting those into strips, and finally cutting the strips into cubes. Let's practice with a potato.

To dice a potato

1. Depending on the size of the potato, cut it two or three times lengthwise (the long way) using the slice method (the cutting method you just learned above). The safest hold for this is the over-the-knife hold. You might need to pull the knife through the potato, keeping the tip on the cutting board. Separate the pieces and put them on their sides so that they are flat.

2. Now, cut these flat pieces lengthwise two or three times with the slice (and pull) method again. Now you have long sticks of potato, like French fries.

3. Finally, keep a few of the sticks close together, and cut them crosswise (the short way) to create cubes. Do the same thing to the rest of the pieces using safe holds on the food and the knife until you have a lot of cubes and nothing else.

The Mince

Now all that's left is the mince, a rocking cut that's used for cutting food into very small pieces. Let's practice mincing an onion.

1. First, dice the onion into small pieces.

2. Now, get all of the onion pieces close together in a little mound.

3. Finally, grip your knife with your dominant hand (the one you write with) and put your free hand on top of the knife blade, near the tip. Try to use a knife that has a slightly curved blade, so that it will rock back and forth. Near the edge of the mound of food, press your knife down. Rock the blade, tip to handle, moving sideways through the food, rocking it the whole time. You can choose how large or small the mince is by how many times you rock the knife through it.

Tips for Using Knives

- Dull knives (excluding butter knives) are more dangerous than sharp knives because dull knives are more likely to slip on the food and cut your finger.
- To keep your knives sharp, all you need is an inexpensive knife sharpener. The most basic type requires that you just pull your knife through a slit in the sharpener.
- Wear goggles when cutting onions to keep your eyes from stinging and getting watery. Swimming goggles will do the trick and keep out those onion gases!
- Whenever you carry a knife, carry it with the point facing down, walk slowly, and watch where you are going.
- For a free knife skills video, check out KidsCookRealFood.com/cookbook.

☆ How to Substitute Ingredients to Make Recipes Allergy-Friendly ☆

By Katie

If you have allergies or food sensitivities, you know how disappointing it can feel to miss out on certain foods because they contain something you can't eat. In this chapter, I will share some tips for adjusting recipes so that you can enjoy them again.

Before we get to that, though, let me tell you my story. My name is Katie, and a couple of years ago I started feeling really sick after eating some of my mama's homemade pork sausage. Eventually, I found out that a tick bite caused me to become allergic to mammal meat (beef, pork, lamb, deer) and dairy.

If I was the only person I knew with food allergies, I'd feel pretty lonely. But over the years, I've made friends who have different limitations because of food allergies. One of my good friends has a bad nut allergy. It's serious enough that his school banned three different nuts from all snacks and lunches so he would be safe. Another friend in my neighborhood who loves to cook is allergic to gluten and dairy. She doesn't let that stop her from cooking, though. She substitutes dairy-free and gluten-free ingredients and still has a great time in the kitchen!

So now you know you're not alone. Here are some tips for making adjustments to some of your favorite recipes so that you can enjoy them again.

DAIRY SUBSTITUTES

There are a lot of good, dairy-free choices for cheese, yogurt, butter, and milk sold at health food stores and even some grocery stores, but there are also some simple substitutions you can make at home. Here are your best bets for milk and butter.

Easy Recipe Substitutes for Milk

Full-fat coconut milk makes a great substitute for milk or cream. You can use it in exact measurements, so if the recipe calls for 1 cup of milk, use 1 cup of coconut milk.

Nut milk, like almond and hazelnut milk, can also work as a substitute for cow's milk. These milks don't have as much fat as coconut milk, though, so they are not as creamy. If you want the recipe to be creamy and you can't use coconut milk, try blending nut milk with some oil. For example, if a recipe calls for 1 cup of cream, but all you have is almond milk and you want the recipe to be creamy, you could try using a little less almond milk, say ¾ cup, and add ¼ cup of avocado oil or olive oil to it. The oil will make the almond milk creamier and less watery.

Something to keep in mind, though, is that an oil with a strong flavor can change the flavor of the recipe. Some olive oils have a spicy, peppery flavor that would probably not taste good in cookies. In that case, choose a more neutral-flavored oil, like avocado oil, or leave the oil out and just use 1 cup of nut milk.

Easy Recipe Substitutes for Butter

There are dairy-free options for butter at the grocery store that have pretty good flavor and healthy ingredients, but in a pinch, here are some options: coconut oil, ghee, and palm kernel oil are all rich in saturated fat, which is the kind of fat that makes butter solid.

Coconut oil doesn't taste anything like butter, but you can use it exactly as you would butter in just about any baking recipe.

Ghee is actually made from butter, but it's filtered to remove the proteins that most people react to, so some people who can't eat butter can have ghee. If you can have ghee, there are some wonderful benefits to using it. Ghee contains vitamins A, D, E and K2, which can help you grow up healthy and strong.

Palm kernel oil (not palm fruit oil) works well as a butter replacement, but there are some negative environmental issues associated with it—some companies harvest palm oil in a way that takes homes away from orangutans and other forest animals. Look for companies that sell sustainably harvested palm oil that doesn't harm forests or the creatures that live in them.

EGG SUBSTITUTES

Many recipes for bread, muffins, cookies, and other yummy creations call for eggs, which is a bummer if you can't have them. Luckily, there are egg substitutes that keep things moist and delicious. There are two very important things you need to know: Egg substitutes usually work best when there are 1–3 eggs in the recipe. If there are more eggs than that, it's probably best to skip the recipe. Deciding which egg substitute works best in a specific recipe may take some experimentation. If you're not sure which one to try first, it might be a good idea to ask an adult for their opinion.

Egg Substitute Options (*each equals one egg*)

Nut butter or seed butter—Use ¼ cup for each egg. Almond butter, sunflower seed butter, macadamia nut butter, cashew butter, walnut butter, pecan butter, tahini, peanut butter, and hazelnut butter are all good options. Don't use crunchy nut butter because it will affect the texture of your recipe.

Applesauce—Use ⅓ cup for each egg. If you are baking bread, muffins, or cake and want a lighter, fluffier texture, add ½ teaspoon of baking powder for every egg substituted.

Pumpkin purée—Use ⅓ cup for each egg. If you are baking bread, muffins, or cake and want a lighter, fluffier texture, add ½ teaspoon of baking powder for every egg substituted.

Flaxseed "egg"—To make the "egg," stir together 1 tablespoon of ground flaxseed with 3 tablespoons of water. Let the mixture sit for 10 minutes before adding to the recipe.

Chia seed "egg"—To make the "egg," stir together 1 tablespoon of chia seeds with 3 tablespoons of water. Let it sit for 10 minutes before adding to the recipe.

Agar "egg"—To make the "egg," stir together 1 tablespoon of agar with 3 tablespoons of water. Let it sit for 15 minutes before adding to the recipe. (If you've never heard of agar before, it's made from seaweed.)

Mashed banana—To make the "egg," mash a banana in a bowl. You will need ¼ cup mashed banana for every egg substituted. If there's any mashed banana left over, try using it in a smoothie. If you are baking bread, muffins, or cake and want a lighter, fluffier texture, add ½ teaspoon of baking powder for every mashed banana in the recipe.

NUT SUBSTITUTES

Almond flour and nut butter are used a lot in gluten-free recipes, which can be tricky if you're also sensitive to almonds or another kind of nut. Here are some ideas that may help.

Easy Recipe Substitute for Almond Flour

If you're allergic or sensitive to almonds, you can use sun flour, which is flour made from ground sunflower seeds. Something you should know, however, is that if you mix sun flour with something acidic like baking soda or lemon juice, your recipe might turn bright green or blue—yeah, you heard me right! It's caused by a chemical reaction between the sunflower and the acid, but even if it happens, the recipe is still totally safe to eat.

Easy Substitute for Nut Butters

If you need to avoid nuts entirely, try using sunflower seed butter instead.

If you are sensitive to just one nut—peanuts, for example—but can have other nuts, one option is to use another nut butter. Experiment with the nut butter you like, and find what works best in your favorite recipes.

SOY SUBSTITUTES

If you are sensitive to soy sauce, try coconut aminos instead. The flavor is a little sweeter than regular soy sauce and super yummy! Teriyaki sauce also sometimes contains soy, and you can use coconut aminos as a replacement for it, too.

CORN SUBSTITUTES

If a recipe calls for corn tortillas, it's pretty easy to use a different kind of tortilla instead, but sometimes corn shows up in less obvious places. Did you know that baking powder sometimes contains corn? To make a corn-free version at home, combine 2 tablespoons of baking soda, 4 tablespoons of cream of tartar, and 2 tablespoons of arrowroot starch or tapioca starch.

Also, if a recipe asks for cornstarch, try arrowroot or tapioca starch instead. We'll talk more about those in the following section.

WHEAT FLOUR SUBSTITUTES

Finding substitutes for wheat flour is difficult, and it is impossible to name one that will work all of the time. Below are some guidelines to try, depending on how the flour is used in a particular recipe. Basically, certain substitutions work better in baking recipes, while others work better as thickeners in other types of recipes.

Gluten-Free Flour Substitutes for Baking

Almond flour—If a recipe calls for 1 cup of wheat flour, try adding ¾–1 cup of almond flour instead. Almond flour doesn't hold recipes together like regular flour does, though, so you might also try adding an extra egg.

Coconut flour—My mom calls coconut flour a "thirsty flour" because it soaks up a lot of liquid. Use about ¼ cup of coconut flour for every 1 cup of wheat flour in a recipe. You'll also want to add about ¼ cup of egg or egg substitute.

Gluten-Free Flour Substitutes for Thickening

Arrowroot starch—Arrowroot is a wonderful thickener, but if you cook it too long, it loses its thickening superpowers. Always add it near the end of cooking.

Tapioca starch—You can usually use tapioca starch the exact same way as arrowroot starch.

Breakfast

Chia Pudding >>> 27

Scrambled Eggs >>> 28

Flourless Banana Split Pancakes >>> 31

Tiramisu French Toast >>> 32

School Day Blueberry Pancakes >>> 35

Breakfast Burritos >>> 36

Crêpes >>> 38

Oven-Baked Eggs & Bacon >>> 40

Oven Pancake >>> 41

Baked Oatmeal Squares >>> 43

Texas-Style Breakfast Tacos >>> 44

Breakfast Casserole >>> 45

Turkey Breakfast Sausage >>> 47

blueberries are good
for your brain!

CHIA PUDDING

By Abigail

Skill > Easy

This is like gelatin, except nothing like gelatin. Well, it's got that gelatin-like feel, but the taste is different. Let's just say it's awesome.

ACTIVE TIME: 10 minutes > TOTAL TIME: 10 minutes plus overnight > MAKES: 4 servings

EQUIPMENT

4 small (1-cup) Mason jars with lids or mugs

Measuring cups and spoons

Small mixing bowl

Mixing spoon

Plastic wrap (if using mugs)

INGREDIENTS

1 can full-fat coconut milk

¼ cup chia seeds

¼ cup blueberries

1 tablespoon honey

1 teaspoon vanilla

1. Arrange the Mason jars or mugs on your counter.

2. In a small mixing bowl, add all the ingredients and stir with the mixing spoon until combined, making sure that there aren't any big chunks of chia seeds or coconut milk remaining. It should be a fairly smooth mixture, but remember, it will have blueberries and chia seeds in it, so it won't look as smooth as milk or another liquid. It should be fairly thick.

3. Pour the same amount of this mixture into each jar and wipe up any drips that you made when you were pouring. Screw the lids onto the jars (or cover the mugs with plastic wrap).

4. Put the jars in the refrigerator until the pudding is chilled and firm, at least 8 hours or overnight.

5. Serve with a smoothie, juice, milk, or water.

SCRAMBLED EGGS

By Abigail

Skill > Moderate

Delicious! This is the perfect egg recipe because it's not boring, and it's not too complicated.

ACTIVE TIME: 15 minutes > TOTAL TIME: 15 minutes > MAKES: 5 servings

EQUIPMENT

Frying pan

2 cereal bowls

Measuring spoons

Butter knife

Whisk or fork

Spatula or wooden spoon

INGREDIENTS

6 free-range eggs

2 tablespoons butter for the pan, plus more as you cook the eggs

2 tablespoons whipping cream

4½ teaspoons of pizza herb mix (just basil is also fine)

Salt to taste

1. Put a frying pan on a burner on the stove.

2. Using two cereal bowls, separate the eggs, allowing the whites (the clear part) to drop into one bowl and the yolks (the yellow part) to drop into the other bowl. (See the box on the next page to learn how to separate the eggs.)

3. Turn the burner under the frying pan to low heat. Using a butter knife, put 2 tablespoons of the butter in the pan to melt.

4. Meanwhile, add the whipping cream to the yolks, and whisk them together with a whisk or a fork until the color has turned a lighter yellow and it is smooth and creamy.

5. When the butter in the frying pan is melted, add the pizza herb mix to the butter and stir with a spatula or wooden spoon to combine. Increase the heat under the frying pan to medium heat.

6. Whisk the egg yolks once more to make sure the cream is incorporated (fully mixed in), and pour the yolks into the frying pan with the butter and herbs. Now sprinkle in a little salt and gently stir.

7. Once the yolks firm up a bit and look like scrambled eggs, pour in the egg whites. Let them cook, without stirring, for 2 minutes.

8. Now stir together the egg whites and yolks while they cook, gently chopping them up with the spatula or wooden spoon as you go, until they are almost cooked.

9. Reduce the heat to low, then add some more butter and keep stirring the eggs so they don't burn. Feel free to add more salt if you think it needs it. Cook the eggs for another 3–4 minutes, then serve.

TO SEPARATE AN EGG

You will need two small bowls. The goal here is to end up with the egg yolks in one bowl and the egg whites in another. Working over the bowl for the egg whites, tap the middle of the egg on the edge of the bowl, then, using two hands, dig into the shell with your thumbs to open up the egg. Trap the yolk in one eggshell half and let the whites in the other eggshell half fall into the bowl. Now, still working over the bowl with the egg whites, transfer the yolk back and forth between your eggshell halves, allowing all the remaining whites to fall into the bowl. Now, dump the yolk into its own bowl.

naturally gluten-free!

Flourless Banana Split Pancakes

By Abigail

Skill > Moderate

If you are looking for a gluten-free breakfast item, this is it. Bananas and eggs take the place of flour, and it tastes—cue the singsong voice—amAzING!

ACTIVE TIME: 45 minutes > **TOTAL TIME: 45 minutes** > **MAKES: 6 servings**

Equipment

Large mixing bowl

Measuring spoons

Whisk or mixing spoon

Food processor

Large frying pan

Butter knife

Spatula to flip the pancakes

Ingredients

6 large bananas, ripe to overripe, mashed

8 eggs

1 teaspoon apple cider vinegar

1 teaspoon nutmeg

½ teaspoon baking powder

4–6 tablespoons butter to cook the pancakes, plus more for serving

Maple syrup or mixed berries for serving

1. In a large mixing bowl, whisk together the bananas, eggs, apple cider vinegar, nutmeg, and baking powder until combined well.

2. Put a food processor on the counter. Dump the banana mixture into the food processor, put the lid on tightly, and process until the batter is creamy.

3. Put a frying pan on a burner on the stove and turn the burner to low heat. Using a butter knife, put 1 tablespoon of butter in the pan to melt.

4. Now it is time to form and cook your pancakes in batches. Using a measuring spoon, pour 2 tablespoons of batter into the butter in the frying pan to form a pancake, and then continue to form as many pancakes as will fit comfortably in the pan. Cook the pancakes until they are brown on the bottom. (To make sure that you aren't burning them, check the bottoms every minute or so with a spatula.) Using the spatula, flip them over and continue to cook until the other side is brown. Transfer the pancakes to a serving platter and make more pancakes in the same way, adding a tablespoon of butter to the pan each time.

5. Serve the pancakes with maple syrup, butter, or berries.

TIRAMISU FRENCH TOAST

By Anthony

Skill > Moderate

Who doesn't love French toast? But have you ever had tiramisu? I've combined both here, but left out the coffee, so it's kid approved. Yum!

ACTIVE TIME: 25 minutes > TOTAL TIME: 25 minutes > MAKES: 6 servings

EQUIPMENT

Serrated knife

Medium and small mixing bowls

Measuring cups and spoons

Whisk

Griddle or frying pan

Spatula

INGREDIENTS

FOR THE FRENCH TOAST

1 large loaf organic bread or French bread

8 eggs

1½ cups milk or cream

1 tablespoon vanilla extract

½ teaspoon almond extract (optional)

1 tablespoon cinnamon

1 tablespoon unsweetened cocoa powder

Salt to taste

FOR THE MASCARPONE CREAM

½ cup mascarpone cheese

1½ cups cup heavy whipping cream

¼ cup maple syrup, plus more for serving

1. Preheat the oven to 375°F.

2. Prepare the French toast and soaking liquid: Using a serrated knife, cut the bread into ½-inch-thick slices. In a medium bowl, combine the eggs, milk or cream, vanilla extract, almond extract (if using), cinnamon, cocoa powder, and salt, and whisk until smooth.

3. Make the mascarpone cream: Clean and dry the whisk. In a small bowl, whisk together the mascarpone cheese, cream, and maple syrup until combined. The mixture will be dense. (You can also use a food processor or immersion blender for a creamier mixture.) Store in the refrigerator until ready to use.

4. Now you are ready to cook the French toast in batches. Put a griddle or frying pan on a burner on the stove and turn the burner to high heat. When the griddle or pan is hot, dip a piece of bread into the egg mixture, making sure both sides are soaked with the mixture, and then place it on the griddle or pan. Coat and place as many pieces of bread as will fit in the griddle or pan. Cook the bread pieces about 2 minutes, until the undersides are lightly browned, then flip with a spatula and cook about 2 minutes more. Coat and cook the remaining bread in the same way, transferring the cooked French toast to a serving plate or individual plates.

5. Serve with a drizzle of maple syrup and some of the mascarpone cream mixture.

School Day Blueberry Pancakes

By Will

Do you ever wake up on a school day and think, "I want pancakes?" Luckily, I have this quick and easy recipe for you, especially if you make the pancakes in advance and reheat them in a pan.

ACTIVE TIME: 30 minutes > TOTAL TIME: 30 minutes > MAKES: 6 servings

EQUIPMENT

Large mixing bowl

Measuring cups and spoons

Mixing spoon

Griddle or large frying pan

Butter knife

Spatula for flipping the pancakes

INGREDIENTS

3 cups sprouted wheat flour

4½ teaspoons baking powder

¾ teaspoon coarse sea salt

3 eggs

3 cups milk

About 12 tablespoons butter for cooking the pancakes, plus more for serving

1½ cups blueberries, frozen or fresh

Maple syrup, for serving

1. In a large bowl, mix together the sprouted wheat flour, baking powder, sea salt, eggs, and milk with a mixing spoon until smooth.

2. Put a griddle or large frying pan on a burner on the stove and turn the burner to medium heat. Using a butter knife, put 2 tablespoons of the butter on the griddle and heat until it starts to foam.

3. Now you are ready to cook the pancakes in small batches. Fill a ¼ cup measuring cup with batter, then pour the batter onto the griddle to form as many pancakes as will fit. Plop a few blueberries into each pancake as they cook. When bubbles start to surface, flip the pancakes over with a spatula. Continue to cook until they are brown on both sides. Transfer the pancakes to a serving plate, and make more pancakes with the remaining butter and batter in the same manner. You can keep the pancakes warm in the oven set to its lowest temperature while you finish cooking all the pancakes, or you can serve them in batches.

4. Serve the pancakes topped with butter and maple syrup. Use any extra blueberries to garnish the pancakes, and, if you have them, add some fresh raspberries for extra color.

BREAKFAST BURRITOS

By Will

Here's another idea for a school day breakfast. These burritos are easy to make in advance. Just wrap them in aluminum foil, and reheat them in a 350°F oven or toaster oven.

ACTIVE TIME: 40 minutes > **TOTAL TIME: 40 minutes** > **MAKES: 6 servings**

EQUIPMENT

Cutting board

Chef's knife

2 small bowls

Measuring cups and
   spoons

Grater

Large frying pan

Spatula or mixing spoon

Slotted spoon

Large mixing bowl

Butter knife

Whisk

1. On a cutting board, using a chef's knife, peel the onion. Finely chop the onion and bell peppers. Transfer the vegetables to a small bowl and set aside. Finely chop enough cilantro to measure ¾ cup, put in another small bowl, and set aside.

2. Using a grater, shred the cheese on the cutting board and set aside.

3. Put a frying pan on a burner on the stove and turn the heat to medium-high. When the pan is hot, add the sausage and cook, chopping it into clumps with a spatula or mixing spoon, until the meat is brown throughout and doesn't have any pink left in it. Using a slotted spoon, transfer the sausage to a large bowl, keeping the fat in the pan. Set the bowl aside.

4. Using a butter knife, add 1½ tablespoons of the butter to the fat in the frying pan. When the butter is melted, add the onion, bell pepper, sea salt, and black pepper and stir until the veggies begin to soften. Transfer to the bowl with the sausage.

5. In a separate bowl, whisk the eggs.

6. Using the butter knife, put the remaining 1½ tablespoons of butter in the frying pan over medium-high heat. Once it starts to foam, pour in the eggs. When the eggs begin to set on the bottom of the pan, use a spatula to gently lift them away from the sides of the pan. Then, while the eggs are still runny, add the shredded cheese and the cooked sausage and veggies. Continue to cook for 1–2 minutes

Ingredients

¾ onion

1½ red bell peppers

¾ cup cilantro

6 ounces Cheddar cheese

15 ounces bulk breakfast sausage

3 tablespoons butter

1½ teaspoons coarse sea salt

⅓ teaspoon ground black pepper

12 eggs

12 flour tortillas

more, until the eggs are cooked through but still wet. Remove the pan from the heat and stir in the cilantro.

7. To roll the burritos, add an equal amount of filling to the center of each tortilla. First fold the sides inward, then roll them up. Serve immediately, with some salsa, if you like, or see below.

MAKE AHEAD

The beauty of these burritos is that you can make them ahead of time for school day breakfasts. Let the cooked filling cool completely, then fill and roll the burritos. Store them in the fridge, covered, overnight. To reheat: put them on a tray in your oven or toaster oven at 350°F for 5–7 minutes, or you can heat them up in a skillet over medium heat with a lid.

CRÊPES

 BY Will

Skill > Moderate

When I went to France with my family, I discovered crêpes and loved them! So I thought I'd share them with you. They are great for breakfast or dessert.

ACTIVE TIME: 40 minutes > TOTAL TIME: 40 minutes > MAKES: 6 servings

EQUIPMENT

Food processor
   or blender

Measuring cups and
   spoons

8-inch skillet

Butter knife

Tongs or metal spatula

Cutting board

Chef's knife

Saucepan

Citrus juicer

A clean, empty jar for
   storing the preserves

1. Prepare the crêpes: Put a food processor or blender on the counter. Add the egg, milk, sprouted flour, and sea salt to the processor or blender and blend until smooth. The batter should be thinner than pancake batter; add a small amount of additional milk, if necessary, to thin it.

2. Put an 8-inch skillet on a burner on the stove and turn the heat to medium. When the skillet is hot, with a butter knife, add 2 tablespoons of the coconut oil or butter to the pan and melt it, swirling the pan to coat completely. Pour 2 tablespoons of batter into the skillet and swirl it around in the skillet until a very thin layer of batter covers the bottom. The crêpe should be about 6 inches in diameter.

3. Cook the crêpe about 30 seconds, or until the batter is bubbly and cooked around the edges. Using tongs or a spatula, flip over the crêpe and cook the other side for about 10 seconds, or until done. Turn the crêpe out onto a clean, dry plate, and make more crêpes with the remaining coconut oil or butter and the batter in the same way.

4. Make the preserves: On a cutting board, with a chef's knife, pit and chop the apricots and transfer to a small saucepan. Using a citrus juicer, juice the lemon and add to the saucepan along with the honey.

FOR THE CRÊPES

2 eggs

2 cups milk, plus more
  if necessary

1½ cups sprouted flour

⅓ teaspoon coarse sea salt

6 tablespoons coconut oil
  or butter

FOR THE APRICOT
PRESERVES

10½ apricots

1½ lemons

3 tablespoons honey

⅓ cup filtered water

2 teaspoons gelatin

5. Put the saucepan on a burner on the stove, and cook the apricot mixture over medium heat, for 20 minutes, stirring frequently. Remove the pan from the burner.

6. Put the cold filtered water into a small bowl, sprinkle the gelatin over it, and stir to combine. Add to the fruit and mix well.

7. Serve the crêpes spread with the preserves.

MAKE AHEAD INFO

It is okay to make the crêpes up to a few days in advance. Cover them tightly with plastic wrap, and refrigerate until ready to serve. The apricot preserves also may be made ahead of time. Just transfer to a clean, empty jar and store in the fridge.

Oven-Baked Eggs & Bacon

By Abigail

My mom taught me how to make this recipe. It's easy and delicious, and it has bacon. You can't get better than that.

ACTIVE TIME: 10 minutes > TOTAL TIME: 17 minutes > MAKES: 5 servings

Equipment

Medium casserole dish
Oven mitts

Ingredients

Butter to grease the
    casserole dish
5 eggs
1 pound bacon
Salt and pepper, to taste

1. Preheat the oven to 350°F and grease the casserole dish with butter.

2. Crack the eggs into a medium casserole dish (see the box below for instructions), making sure each yolk has its own little space and they are not on top of each other.

3. Lay the strips of bacon on top of the eggs. Try not to lay the pieces on top of each other if you can help it. If all the pieces in one package don't fit in your oven dish, leave out the ones that don't.

4. Wearing oven mitts, transfer the casserole to the hot oven and bake for 7 minutes.

5. Wearing oven mitts, remove the casserole from the oven, and transfer it to a cool burner on the stovetop. Let cool for 5 minutes.

6. Sprinkle with salt and pepper, to taste, and serve.

HOW TO CRACK AN EGG

Lightly tap the egg on the counter or on the edge of a bowl. Then, over a bowl or pan, dig your thumbs into the shell and pull it apart. The egg will fall into the bowl.

OVEN PANCAKE

BY Abigail   *Skill* > Advanced

This is *amazing* with real Canadian maple syrup (and we happen to live in the heart of Canada, so we get the good stuff) and super-duper easy to make. Just mix, oven, done!

ACTIVE TIME: 10 minutes > TOTAL TIME: 35 minutes > MAKES: 2–3 servings

EQUIPMENT

10-inch cast-iron skillet

Measuring cups and spoons

Mixing bowl

Mixing spoon

Oven mitts

INGREDIENTS

2 tablespoons butter

3 extra-large eggs, at room temperature

½ cup plus 2 tablespoons whole milk

½ cup gluten-free all-purpose flour blend

Pinch of salt

Maple syrup, berries, or butter, for serving

1. Preheat the oven to 375°F. Coat a skillet with the butter.

2. Put the eggs, milk, gluten-free flour blend, and salt in a mixing bowl and stir with a mixing spoon until combined well and no lumps remain. Transfer to the buttered skillet.

3. Wearing oven mitts, transfer the skillet to the hot oven, and bake the pancake for 25 minutes, or until puffed up and slightly golden. (If the pancake needs more time to bake, set a timer for another 3 minutes and check again. Do this until it's golden and puffed up.)

4. Serve with maple syrup, berries, or just butter.

Tip

You can double or triple this recipe. My family triples it, although we always want more, so we're starting to quadruple it.

Tip

It's the pectin in the blueberries that keeps the oatmeal together in this recipe. Pectin is like a sort of healthy gelatin. It's in other things as well, but blueberries are full of pectin. Taking the blueberries away would make these squares crumbly and hard to hold.

Baked Oatmeal Squares

By Abigail

Skill > Advanced

Oatmeal with blueberries! Try. The. Recipe. NOW!

ACTIVE TIME: 10 minutes > TOTAL TIME: 55 minutes > MAKES: 6 servings

Equipment

Small saucepan

Measuring cups and
spoons

Small bowl

Whisk or a fork

Oven-safe casserole dish
at least 1½ inches deep

Spatula or mixing spoon

Oven mitts

Ingredients

1 cup (2 sticks) butter
or coconut oil

4 eggs

6 cups rolled oats

4 teaspoons baking
powder

1 teaspoon salt

1 teaspoon cinnamon

2 cups cultured milk
product, such as
buttermilk, yogurt,
or milk.

¾ cup honey

2 cups frozen blueberries

1. Preheat the oven to 350°F.

2. Put a small saucepan on a burner on the stove and turn the heat to low. Add the butter or coconut oil and melt, stirring occasionally. (Don't let the butter burn!) Turn off the heat and remove the pan from the heat. Let the butter cool.

3. Crack the eggs into a small bowl and use a whisk or a fork to beat them together.

4. Place a casserole dish that's at least 1½ inches deep on the counter. Add the oats, baking powder, salt, cinnamon, cultured milk product, honey, cooled melted butter, and the beaten eggs and stir together with a spatula or mixing spoon until combined well. Carefully stir in the frozen blueberries. Using a spatula, even out the mixture in the casserole.

5. Wearing oven mitts, place the oven dish in the hot oven and cook the casserole for 35–40 minutes, or until it is golden brown on top.

6. Wearing oven mitts, transfer the casserole to a cool burner on the stove and let the oatmeal cool for a few minutes.

7. Cut into squares and serve.

Texas-Style Breakfast Tacos

By Anthony   Skill > Advanced

My mom grew up in Texas, where they serve breakfast tacos a lot, so these have always been part of my life. They're fun for a family because each person can customize their own taco. My brother and I sometimes add hot sauce, but my sisters like sour cream and cheese.

ACTIVE TIME: 30 minutes > TOTAL TIME: 30 minutes > MAKES: 6–8 servings

Equipment

Large skillet

Spatula

Plates for the fillings and toppings

Butter knife

Measuring spoons

Ingredients

8 ounces precooked hash browns or potatoes

1 pound breakfast sausage (turkey, pork, or chicken all work)

1 tablespoon butter

6 eggs

½ teaspoon salt

½ teaspoon pepper

8 corn tortillas (or 6-inch flour tortillas)

1 cup shredded cheese

Salsa, sour cream, or sliced onions, for topping

1. Put a large skillet on a burner on the stove and turn the heat to medium-high. When the skillet is hot, add the sausage and cook, turning with a spatula, until browned. Transfer the sausage to a plate and set it aside.

2. Use the same skillet to cook the eggs. Reduce the heat to medium. Using a butter knife, transfer the butter to the skillet and melt the butter in the pan. Carefully crack the eggs into the skillet and add salt and pepper. Cook, stirring gently, until the eggs are cooked, but still soft and fluffy. Transfer to a serving platter.

3. Let everyone in your family assemble their own breakfast tacos with the tortillas, hash browns, sausage, eggs, shredded cheese, and preferred toppings.

Tip

If you don't use all of the filling ingredients, save them to make an omelet or quiche another day.

BREAKFAST CASSEROLE

By Anthony · **Skill > Advanced**

This breakfast casserole (my grandma's recipe) is a good source of protein. I like to prep it the night before so I can wake up early and make it for my parents to surprise them.

ACTIVE TIME: 15 minutes > TOTAL TIME: 1 hour > MAKES: 6–8 servings

EQUIPMENT

Large mixing bowl

Measuring cups and spoons

Mixing spoon

Large skillet

Spatula

Medium bowl for beating eggs

Fork

9- by 13-inch baking dish

INGREDIENTS

1 cup all-purpose flour (or 1¼ cup Cassava flour)

2 teaspoons baking powder

1 teaspoon dried mustard powder

½ teaspoon salt

½ teaspoon pepper

1 pound bulk breakfast sausage (pork, turkey and chicken all work)

8 eggs

2 cups milk (whole milk and coconut milk both work)

1 cup grated cheese

1 tablespoon butter for greasing the baking dish

1. In a large mixing bowl, add the flour, baking powder, mustard powder, salt, and pepper and mix together with a mixing spoon to combine. Set aside.

2. Put a large skillet on a burner on the stove and turn the heat to medium-high. When the skillet is hot, add the bulk sausage and cook it, chopping it up in small pieces with a spatula, until it is brown all the way through with no pink remaining.

3. Crack the eggs into a medium bowl and beat them with a fork. Add them to the bowl with the flour, then add the milk and stir well with the spatula or a mixing spoon to combine. Now add the cheese and sausage and stir together until everything is combined well. Cover the bowl and store in the refrigerator until you're ready to bake and serve the casserole (up to 24 hours).

4. When ready to cook, preheat the oven to 350°F. Grease a 9- by 13-inch baking dish or 8- by 8-inch baking dish with the butter.

5. Dump the egg and sausage mixture into the prepared baking dish and use a spatula to spread it out evenly. Wearing oven mitts, place the baking dish in the hot oven and bake the casserole for 45–50 minutes, or until a fork inserted into the center comes out clean.

EQUIPMENT LESSON

A rimmed baking sheet is a flat baking sheet with a little wall or lip around the edges. Sometimes sausage makes a lot of juice while baking, and the rim keeps the juices from dripping off the edge. Parchment paper is used to line your baking sheet. It keeps foods from sticking to the sheet, making clean-up that much easier.

Tip

These sausages are delicious with maple syrup, or you can use them with my "Cornbread" Muffins (on page 163) to make them into breakfast sandwiches with cheese. **Yum!**

Turkey Breakfast Sausage

By Katie

I love my mama's stovetop sausage, but when I was learning to cook I didn't like getting splattered by oil. To solve the problem I started making mine in the oven.

ACTIVE TIME: 10 minutes > TOTAL TIME: 33–36 minutes > MAKES: 4 servings

EQUIPMENT

Rimmed baking sheet
Parchment paper
Medium mixing bowl
Fork
Measuring spoons
Oven mitts

INGREDIENTS

1 pound ground turkey
2 tablespoons maple syrup or honey
1½ teaspoons ground sage
1½ teaspoons dried thyme
½ teaspoon salt
¼ teaspoon marjoram
Avocado oil or olive oil for coating your hands
Maple syrup, for serving

1. Preheat the oven to 400°F. Line a rimmed baking sheet with parchment paper.

2. In a medium bowl, add the turkey, maple syrup or honey, sage, thyme, salt, and marjoram and mix together with a fork.

3. To form the patties, rub your hands with a little bit of oil to prevent the mixture from sticking (or at least reduce it). Using a measuring spoon, scoop out 2 tablespoons of the turkey mixture and form it into a patty with your hands. Place the patty on the lined baking sheet. Make more patties with the remaining turkey mixture the same way, placing them on the sheet about 1 inch apart. Wash your hands.

4. Wearing oven mitts, transfer the baking sheet to the hot oven and bake the sausage patties for 20 minutes. Then turn the oven on broil and continue cooking for 3–6 minutes to brown the sausage patties on top. Wear your oven mitts to remove the rimmed baking sheet to a cool burner on the top of the stove, and check to make sure the sausages are cooked through. If they are not, reduce the oven temperature back to 400°F and continue to bake the sausages until they are done.

5. Wearing oven mitts, carefully transfer the hot baking sheet to a cool burner on the stove.

6. Drizzle the sausages with maple syrup and serve immediately.

Lunch

Cucumber Salad >>> 50

Strawberry-Pecan Salad >>> 53

Apple Sandwiches >>> 55

Lentil Soup >>> 57

Mac 'n' Cheese >>> 59

Avocado Chicken Salad >>> 60

Taco Salad >>> 62

BLTA Sandwich >>> 64

Pasta Salad >>> 65

Avocado Quesadilla >>> 67

Bacon Tomato Soup >>> 68

Easy Chicken Avocado Soup >>> 71

Black Bean Soup >>> 72

Creamed Cauliflower >>> 74

Egg Drop Soup >>> 77

Egg Fried Rice >>> 78

Cheeseburger Casserole >>> 80

Taco Casserole >>> 82

Tomato, Zucchini, & Mozzarella Bake >>> 84

Margherita Pizza >>> 85

Chicken Ranch Wraps with Greek Yogurt Ranch Dressing >>> 88

Baked Fish Sticks with Tartar Sauce >>> 90

Best Burger with Secret Yum Sauce >>> 92

CUCUMBER SALAD

By Abigail

Skill > Moderate

You know what's amazing? Greek salad made with crunchy cucumbers, salty feta, red onion, and pitted olives! I'm not a tomato fan, so I usually just cut up a few and serve them on the side to keep a few of my family members happy . . . it's up to you.

ACTIVE TIME: 20 minutes > TOTAL TIME: 20 minutes > MAKES: 6 servings

EQUIPMENT

Cutting board

Chef's knife

Medium salad bowl

Paring knife

Measuring cups and spoons

Serrated knife (if using tomatoes)

1. Using a cutting board and a chef's knife, cut the cucumbers, one at a time, into bite-size dice (small cubes). To do this, cut one of the cucumbers lengthwise in half. Put the flat (cut sides) down on the board, then cut each piece lengthwise in half again. Now put two strips together and cut them crosswise into bite-size dice (small squares). Cut the remaining strips in the same way. Transfer the dice to a salad bowl. Cut up the remaining cucumber in the same way. Transfer the dice to the bowl.

2. Using the cutting board and the chef's knife, cut the piece of feta into bite-size dice, about the same size as your cucumber dice. To do this, cut the piece of feta lengthwise in half, then cut each half lengthwise in half again. Now cut it all up crosswise into the dice and transfer to the salad bowl.

3. Using a small paring knife, peel off the papery outside of the chilled onion. Using the cutting board and the paring knife, carefully chop off each end (the root end and the top end). Now, using a chef's knife in your dominant hand (the hand you write with), hold the onion with your other hand (fingers carefully tucked in, see page 18) and slice up the onion into thin rounds. Lay the rounds flat on the board and cut them in half. With your hands, separate the pieces and transfer them to the salad bowl.

INGREDIENTS

FOR THE SALAD

2 cucumbers

Approximately 6 ounces feta (enough for 1½ cups of small dice)

1 red onion, chilled

1 cups pitted olives

4 medium tomatoes (optional)

FOR THE DRESSING

3 tablespoons olive oil

1 tablespoon red wine vinegar

1 minced garlic clove

1 teaspoon dried oregano

4. Using the paring knife, peel and mince the garlic and set it aside.

5. Add the pitted olives to the bowl.

6. If your family likes tomatoes, use a serrated knife to cut a few up on the cutting board, and add them to the salad bowl (or put them in a separate serving bowl).

7. Add the olive oil, red wine vinegar, garlic, and oregano to the salad bowl, toss until everything is coated, then serve the salad.

Tip

To make full meal, you can add some
leftover grilled or roasted chicken.

STRAWBERRY-PECAN SALAD

By Anthony

Skill > Easy

Salads are so healthy, but sometimes they can taste boring. I promise, this one definitely is not boring! The dressing is really easy to make, and it doesn't have vinegar (which a lot of kids think is too strong).

ACTIVE TIME: 10 minutes > TOTAL TIME: 10 minutes > MAKES: 6–8 servings

EQUIPMENT

Blender

Cutting board

Paring knife

Measuring cup and spoons

Citrus juicer

Small skillet

Mixing spoon

Salad spinner

Medium or large salad bowl

Salad tongs

INGREDIENTS

1 pound strawberries

1 lemon

¼ cup olive oil

2 tablespoons maple syrup

8 ounces pecans

Pinch of salt

8 ounces spinach

1. *Make the dressing:* Put a blender on the counter. On a cutting board with a small paring knife, cut off the green part of the strawberry, and cut up enough into small pieces to measure 1 cup. Transfer to the blender. Cut the lemon in half, juice the lemon with a citrus juicer, and pour the juice into the blender. Add the olive oil and 1 tablespoon of the maple syrup and blend the mixture until smooth. Set the dressing aside.

2. Put a small skillet on a burner on the stove. Add the pecans to the skillet and turn the heat to medium-high. Using a mixing spoon, gently stir the nuts for 2 minutes (you will smell a warm, nutty aroma). Add the remaining 1 tablespoon of maple syrup and a pinch of salt and stir for 10 seconds. Turn off the burner and remove the skillet from the heat. Let the pecans cool.

3. Wash the spinach in a large bowl of water and spin it dry in a salad spinner. Transfer the spinach to a salad bowl.

4. Add the cooled pecans to the salad bowl.

5. On the cutting board with a paring knife, slice the remaining strawberries into quarters and add them to the salad bowl with the spinach and pecans. Using salad tongs, gently toss the salad to combine.

6. Pour the dressing over the salad and toss with the salad tongs until everything is coated with the dressing.

APPLE SANDWICHES

By Katie

Skill > Easy

The sweetness of the apple blends perfectly with the sharpness of the Cheddar and the saltiness of the bacon or deli meat in this amazing, perfectly easy sandwich!

ACTIVE TIME: 7 minutes > **TOTAL TIME: 7 minutes** > **MAKES: 3 servings**

EQUIPMENT

Large skillet (if using uncooked bacon)

Tongs (if using uncooked bacon)

Cutting board

Apple corer

Medium utility knife

Serving plate

INGREDIENTS

About 4–8 slices bacon or turkey bacon, or 6 slices of deli meat (or both)

½ teaspoon avocado or olive oil (if using turkey bacon)

1 large apple

1–2 lemon wedges, if needed

About 3 ounces Cheddar cheese or dairy-free cheese

1. If using the bacon, put a large skillet on a burner on the stove and turn the heat to high. If you're using turkey bacon, add ½ teaspoon oil to the skillet. When the skillet is hot, add the bacon and cook, turning once with tongs, until crisp and brown on both sides. Set aside.

2. Working on a cutting board and using an apple corer, remove the core from the apple. Then, using a medium utility knife, slice the apple into about six flat pieces (it's okay if you have a little more or a little less). If you are not going to eat the apple immediately, rub a lemon wedge over the cut sides of the apple slices to keep them from turning brown. Place half of the apple slices on a serving plate. Set aside the remaining slices.

3. Top the apple slices on the serving plate with the cooked bacon and/or deli meat, dividing it equally.

4. Working on the cutting board with a medium utility knife, cut the cheese into thin slices. Top the bacon (and/or deli meat) with the cheese, dividing it equally.

5. Top the cheese with the remaining apple slices to complete the "sandwiches."

LENTIL SOUP

By Abigail   **Skill** > Moderate

Ever been to Turkey? Turkey has so many amazing things—the people, the culture, the cleanliness, and the *food*! Baklava, Turkish delight (yes, it's very Turkishly delightful!), hummus, and especially lentil soup.

ACTIVE TIME: 10 minutes > TOTAL TIME: 35 minutes > MAKES: 5 servings

EQUIPMENT

Blender
Large pot
Measuring cups
Cutting board
Chef's knife
Mixing spoon
Small spoon, for tasting

INGREDIENTS

1 tomato

6 cups chicken broth (canned or homemade, page 97)

3 carrots

1 onion

Fresh parsley (to measure ½ cup chopped)

1½ cups lentils

Salt to taste

Sour cream, cheese, extra parsley, chopped green onions, or tortilla chips, for serving

1. Put the blender on the counter. Add the tomato to the blender, put the lid on tightly, and blend on medium speed for about 5–10 seconds, until it looks like a chunky soup (but not too chunky). Set aside.

2. Put a large pot on a burner on the stove and turn the heat to high. Add the broth and let it heat up.

3. Meanwhile, working on a cutting board with a chef's knife, chop the carrots into small pieces. Peel and chop the onion into small pieces. Chop enough of the parsley to measure ½ cup and add it to the broth. Add the carrots and onions to the broth.

4. Add the blended tomato mixture and the lentils to the vegetable mixture in the pot, and stir with a mixing spoon to combine. Bring the mixture to a boil, then reduce the heat to low heat and simmer until the lentils start to puff up a bit and become tender, about 13–14 minutes. (To test for doneness, take a small spoon and taste the soup, but remember that the mixture is hot, so don't burn your tongue. If the lentils are still too hard, keep tasting the soup every 4–5 minutes. You can put a lid on the pot to make it cook faster.)

5. When the soup is ready, add salt to taste, if desired.

6. Serve the soup topped with sour cream, cheese, extra parsley, chopped green onions, or tortilla chips.

so delicious!

MAC 'N' CHEESE

By Will

Skill > Moderate

Like most kids, I have loved and adored mac 'n' cheese my whole life. Until a few years ago, I thought it was a restaurant food, and then I realized that I could make it myself.

ACTIVE TIME: 40 minutes > TOTAL TIME: 40 minutes > MAKES: 6 servings

EQUIPMENT

Large pot

Grater

Large colander for draining

Butter knife

Measuring cups and spoons

Oven mitts

Mixing spoon

Butter knife

INGREDIENTS

18 ounces elbow macaroni

18 ounces sharp Cheddar cheese

3 tablespoons Parmesan cheese

3 tablespoons butter

1½ cups milk

¾ cup cream

2¼ teaspoons ground dry mustard

1 teaspoon sea salt

2¼ teaspoons ground black pepper

1. Fill a large pot with water. Put the pot on a burner on the stove and turn the heat to high. Bring the water to a rapid boil, then add the macaroni, and cook according to the instructions on the box.

2. While the pasta is cooking, use a grater to grate the Cheddar and Parmesan cheeses.

3. Set a large colander in the sink. Once the pasta is just tender (but not mushy), carefully remove ½ cup of the pasta water with a liquid measuring cup and set it aside. Wearing oven mitts, carefully carry the pot to the sink and drain the pasta in the large colander (or have an adult do this for you). Rinse the pasta thoroughly with cool water and let it drain. Set aside.

4. Put the same pot back on a burner on the stove and turn the heat to medium. With a butter knife, add the butter to the pot and let it melt. Add the milk, cream, and cheeses, stirring constantly with the mixing spoon, until smooth and creamy. Then mix in the dry mustard, sea salt, and pepper.

5. Add the pasta to the cheese sauce and stir until combined. To thin the sauce, stir in 1 tablespoon of the reserved pasta water at a time until it looks like the perfect consistency.

Avocado Chicken Salad

By Will

Skill > Moderate

For me, avocados are an essential salad ingredient. My mom has always made this salad, and I've always begged for more. Now I can make it for myself whenever I want.

ACTIVE TIME: 30 minutes > TOTAL TIME: 30 minutes > MAKES: 8 servings

Equipment

Skillet
Measuring spoons
Butter knife
Plate
Cutting board
Paring knife
Large bowl
Chef's knife
Citrus juicer
Salad spinner
Large serving bowl
 or plates

1. Put a skillet on a burner on the stove and turn the heat to medium-high. With a butter knife, add the coconut oil, then swirl the pan to coat it. Add the chicken and cook until browned on both sides and cooked through. Turn off the heat and transfer the chicken to a plate to cool.

2. Using a cutting board and a paring knife, peel, pit, and chop the avocado into small pieces (see the box below) and transfer the pieces to a large bowl.

3. Using a chef's knife, mince the green onions and cilantro and transfer to the large bowl with the avocado.

TO CUT, PEEL, SLICE, OR SCOOP OUT AN AVOCADO

Using a paring knife, cut the avocado lengthwise all the way around. Then, taking each half of the avocado in a separate hand, twist until it comes apart. Depending on the ripeness of the avocado, you can now easily peel off the skin if the avocado is firm or scoop out the "meat" with a spoon if it's ripe and soft. To remove the pit, hold the avocado half with the pit in your nondominant hand (the one you don't write with), use the knife in your dominant hand to firmly tap the pit, and lift it out of the avocado meat. (Have an adult do this for you.) Once your avocado is free of skin and pit, thinly slice it.

Ingredients

3 tablespoons coconut oil

2¼ pounds boneless, skinless chicken breasts

4½ large avocados

3 green onions

¾ bunch cilantro

1½ limes

¾ teaspoon garlic powder

1½ teaspoons sea salt, plus more to taste

Ground black pepper to taste

12 ounces baby salad greens

4. Cut the limes into halves. Juice the lime halves with a citrus juicer and add the juice to the avocado mixture.

5. When the chicken is cool, shred it with your hands or use a chef's knife, and dice it into ½-inch cubes. Transfer the chicken to the avocado mixture. Add the garlic powder, sea salt, and black pepper and toss to combine. Season with additional sea salt and pepper to taste.

6. Wash and spin dry the salad greens. Transfer the greens to a large bowl or individual plates, and spoon the avocado and chicken mixture over the greens.

Taco Salad

By Will

Kids typically don't like salads. Until they meet this one.

ACTIVE TIME: 30 minutes > TOTAL TIME: 30 minutes > MAKES: 4 servings

Equipment

Large skillet

Measuring cups and spoons

Spatula

Food processor or blender

Cutting board

Paring knife

Spoons, for scooping avocado and for tasting

Chef's knife

Citrus juicer

Salad spinner

Large salad bowl

Serrated knife

Slotted spoon

Ingredients

FOR THE TACO MEAT

Ghee, or fat of your choice

1½ pounds ground beef

1½ teaspoons sea salt

1 tablespoon chili powder

1½ teaspoons ground cumin

¾ teaspoon paprika

¾ teaspoon garlic powder

¾ teaspoon onion powder

FOR THE DRESSING

1 avocado

1 clove garlic

2 limes

⅓ cup yogurt

3 tablespoons olive oil

1 cup cilantro

2 teaspoons coarse sea salt

Ground black pepper, to taste

Filtered water, as needed to thin

FOR THE SALAD

1 large head of romaine lettuce

2 avocados

6 green onions

1 red bell pepper

1 yellow bell pepper

2 cups cherry tomatoes

2 cups tortilla chips

1. Cook the meat. Put a large skillet on a burner on the stove and turn the heat to medium. Add the ghee or fat of your choice and heat until melted, then add the ground beef, sea salt, chili powder, cumin, paprika, garlic powder, and onion powder and cook, chopping the meat with a spatula, until the meat is cooked through and no pink remains. Turn the heat off and transfer the skillet to a cool burner.

2. Make the dressing. Put a food processor (or a blender) on the counter. Using a cutting board and paring knife, pit and peel the avocado (see the box on page 60) and scoop out the flesh. Peel the garlic clove. Cut the limes in half. Using a citrus juicer, juice the limes. Add the avocado, garlic clove, and lime juice to the food processor with the yogurt, olive oil, cilantro, salt, and pepper. Put the top on the processor and purée the mixture until it is creamy and smooth. Taste a bit of the dressing with a spoon, then add more salt and pepper to taste. Thin with water to desired consistency and set aside.

3. Prepare the salad. Wash the lettuce and spin it dry in a salad spinner. Transfer the lettuce to a large cutting board and, using a chef's knife, chop it into bite-size pieces. Dump the lettuce into a large salad bowl. Next, peel and pit the avocados and cut into small pieces (see the box on page 60). Transfer the avocado pieces to the salad bowl. Now, using the chef's knife, chop the green onions and the bell peppers into small pieces and add them to the salad bowl. Finally, using a serrated knife, cut the tomatoes in half, if desired, and add to the salad.

4. Using a slotted spoon, add the cooked taco meat to the salad bowl and toss the salad with tongs to combine. Finally, add the dressing and toss gently until everything is coated. Top with crushed tortilla chips and serve.

BLTA SANDWICH

 Will

Skill > Moderate

Bacon, lettuce, tomato, avocado—the best things to ever to go into any kind of sandwich.

ACTIVE TIME: 25 minutes > TOTAL TIME: 25 minutes > MAKES: 6 servings

EQUIPMENT

Large skillet

Tongs

Paper towels

Plate for draining
   the bacon

Salad spinner

Cutting board

Serrated knife

Paring knife

Toaster

Butter knife

INGREDIENTS

1½ pounds bacon

1½ heads butter lettuce

6 heirloom tomatoes

3 avocados

12 slices sourdough bread

9 tablespoons butter,
   softened

Mayonnaise

1. Put a large skillet on a burner on the stove and turn the heat to medium. Add the bacon to the hot skillet and cook, turning it over with tongs, until crisp on both sides and cooked through. Put some paper towels on a plate. Transfer the bacon with tongs to the paper towels to drain.

2. Separate the lettuce leaves, wash them, and spin them dry in the salad spinner.

3. Working on a cutting board with a serrated knife, slice the tomatoes thinly and set aside. With a paring knife, pit and peel the avocados (see the box on page 60). Cut the avocados into thin slices.

4. Put a toaster on the counter. Toast the bread and arrange the toasted slices on a large work surface.

5. Using a butter knife, spread the butter and mayonnaise onto the tops of the toasted bread. Stack six slices of the bread with the bacon, lettuce, tomato slices, and avocado slices. Top with the remaining bread and serve.

Pasta Salad

By Paul

I brought this pasta salad to my grandparents' house for our extended family reunion, and it vanished pretty quickly! For a big gathering, it would be a good idea to make a double batch.

ACTIVE TIME: 20–30 minutes > TOTAL TIME: 20–30 minutes > MAKES: about 6 servings

Equipment

Medium pot with lid

Measuring cups and spoons

Cutting board

Chef's knife

Small bowls

Colander

Oven mitts

Large serving bowl

Large mixing spoon

Ingredients

1 tablespoon salt

6 ounces Cheddar cheese (sharp or mild)

1 Roma tomato

Half of a small red bell pepper

15 slices of pepperoni (optional)

2 cups pasta, such as shells or elbow pasta

½ cup frozen or fresh peas

¼ cup Italian dressing

1. Fill a medium pot three-quarters full with water and add the salt. Put the pot on a burner on the stove and turn the heat to high. Cover the pot with a lid and bring the water to a boil.

2. Meanwhile, working on a cutting board and using a chef's knife, prepare the following ingredients. Cut the cheese into small dices (cubes). Cut the Roma tomato into small pieces. Cut the red bell pepper into small dices (cubes). If using the pepperoni, cut the slices into quarters. Place each ingredient into a small bowl.

3. When the water in the pot is boiling, remove the lid. Add the pasta to the pot and cook until just tender according to the box instructions.

4. Put a colander in the sink. When the pasta is done, put on oven mitts and carefully carry the pot to the sink and drain the pasta in the colander (have an adult to do this for you).

5. Dump the hot pasta into a large serving bowl, add the cheese cubes, tomato, bell pepper cubes, pepperoni, peas, and Italian dressing, and stir with a large mixing spoon until combined well.

6. Serve hot or after being chilled in the fridge.

Tip

If you're bringing the salad somewhere, bring extra dressing so you can make sure the salad doesn't dry out!

Tip

If you are making more than 3 or 4 quesadillas at a time and you'd like to keep them warm, you can keep them on a plate in a warm oven (200°F) while you prepare the other quesadillas.

Avocado Quesadilla

By Will   **Skill** > Moderate

This is quick and easy and will never let you down. Heaven.

ACTIVE TIME: 45 minutes > TOTAL TIME: 45 minutes > MAKES: 4–6 servings

---

EQUIPMENT

Cutting board
Paring knife
Grater
Butter knife
Large skillet with a lid
Metal spatula

INGREDIENTS

2 avocados

8 ounces mild
   Cheddar cheese

4 tablespoons butter

1 dozen sprouted
   corn tortillas

Coarse sea salt, to taste

1. Working on a cutting board and using a paring knife, pit, peel, and thinly slice the avocados (see the box on page 60).

2. Using a grater, shred the cheese.

3. Cook and assemble the quesadillas in batches: Put a large skillet on a burner on the stove and turn the heat to medium-high. Using a butter knife, put 2 tablespoons of the butter in the skillet to melt. Once the butter is foaming, place a single layer of tortillas in the pan. Top with some cheese (you'll need to take into account the number of quesadillas you will be making to divvy up the cheese). Cover the skillet and cook until the cheese is melted.

4. Top the cheese with some avocado slices (again you'll need to take into account the number of quesadillas you will be making), a sprinkle of sea salt, and another tortilla. Flip the quesadillas with a spatula so that the browned tortilla is now on top and grill just until the bottom tortilla is softened or lightly browned. Make more quesadillas, as needed, with the remainder of the tortillas and ingredients.

BACON TOMATO SOUP

 Will

Skill > Moderate

Tomato soup is my sister's favorite thing ever, so I decided to switch it up with bacon.

ACTIVE TIME: 20 minutes > TOTAL TIME: 55 minutes > MAKES: 6 servings

EQUIPMENT

Large heavy pot

Tongs

Paper towels

Plate for draining
  the bacon

Cutting board

Chef's knife

Butter knife

Measuring cups and
  spoons

Mixing spoon

Slotted spoon

Immersion blender
  or regular blender

1. Put a large heavy pot on a burner on the stove and turn the heat to medium. Add the bacon and cook, turning it over with tongs until it is crisp on both sides. Turn off the burner under the pan. Line a plate with paper towels. Transfer the bacon to the paper towels to drain. Set aside. Leave the bacon fat in the pan.

2. On a large cutting board with a chef's knife, peel the onions. Coarsely chop the onions, celery, and carrots. Peel and mince the garlic.

3. Turn the burner under the pot to medium heat. With a butter knife, add the butter, onions, celery, carrots, garlic, and sea salt to the fat in the pot, and cook the vegetables, stirring occasionally with a mixing spoon, until soft, about 10 minutes.

4. Add the tomato paste, and cook, stirring, until the mixture is lightly browned, about 3 minutes. Sprinkle in the flour and cook about 2 minutes more.

5. Add the stock, tomatoes, thyme, and bay leaves. Turn the heat down to medium-low and simmer the mixture (only little bubbles should break the surface) for about 30 minutes.

6. Remove the pot from the heat. With a slotted spoon, remove and discard the thyme and bay leaves. Using an immersion blender, purée the soup right in the pan until it is smooth. (Or, if you need to use a regular blender, blend it in very small batches with the funnel

INGREDIENTS

12 slices bacon

1½ onions

1½ stalks celery

1½ carrots

12 cloves garlic

3 tablespoons butter

1½ teaspoons coarse sea
salt, plus more to taste

¼ cup tomato paste

4½ teaspoons sprouted
flour

1½ quarts chicken stock

48 ounces canned diced
tomatoes

3 sprigs fresh thyme

1½ bay leaves

¾ cup heavy cream

Ground black pepper,
to taste

cap off to allow the steam to escape and to avoid burning yourself with exploding hot soup. Use a ladle to transfer a small amount of the soup to the blender and blend it until smooth. Transfer the puréed soup to another clean pan and continue to purée the soup in the same manner until all of the soup is smooth.)

7. Stir in the heavy cream, then season with salt and pepper.

8. Serve the soup garnished with the crispy bacon crumbled on top. (Save any extra bacon for a later meal or snack.)

Easy Chicken Avocado Soup

By Will

Skill > Moderate

My sister and I begged my mom to make us this mouthwatering soup so many times—it's that good. Now we can make it for ourselves!

ACTIVE TIME: 45 minutes > **TOTAL TIME:** 45 minutes > **MAKES: 8 servings**

Equipment

Plate

Cutting board

Chef's knife

Large pot

Measuring cups and spoons

Mixing spoon

Citrus juicer

Small spoon, for tasting

Paring knife

Ingredients

3 cups cooked chicken

1½ bunches green onions

9 cloves garlic

¼ cup extra-virgin olive oil

3 quarts chicken stock (canned or homemade, page 97)

1½ teaspoons coarse sea salt, plus more to taste

4½ limes

4½ avocados

1½ bunches cilantro

1. Shred the chicken with your hands and put it on a plate. Set aside.

2. On a cutting board with a chef's knife, mince the green onions, keeping the white and green parts separate, and peel and mince the garlic cloves.

3. Put a large pot on a burner on the stove and turn the heat to medium. Add the oil and heat until hot but not smoking. Add the white parts of the green onions and cook, stirring with a mixing spoon until almost tender, about 1½ minutes, then add the garlic and cook, stirring constantly for only 30 seconds.

4. Add the chicken stock and sea salt. Increase the heat to medium-high and bring the mixture to a boil.

5. Meanwhile, using a citrus juicer, juice the limes.

6. When the stock mixture comes to a boil, reduce the heat to medium and add the shredded chicken and lime juice. With a small spoon, taste a bit of soup and add more salt if necessary. Continue to cook the soup just until the chicken is warmed through.

7. Meanwhile, working on a cutting board with a paring knife, peel, pit, and dice the avocados (see the box on page 60). With a chef's knife, chop the cilantro into small pieces.

8. Just before serving, stir in the cilantro and the reserved green part of the green onions. Serve the soup topped with the diced avocados.

BLACK BEAN SOUP

By Paul   Skill > Moderate

Black beans are good for you, and when they're combined with lots of spices they are delicious, too. Although this recipe involves slicing, dicing, sautéing, and measuring, it isn't as difficult as it might look.

ACTIVE TIME: 10–15 minutes > TOTAL TIME: 40–55 minutes > MAKES: about 5 servings

EQUIPMENT

Cutting board

Chef's knife

Garlic press

Large pot with lid

Measuring cups and spoons

Large mixing spoon

Colander

Can opener

Immersion blender or regular blender

Tip

Crushing garlic and letting it rest before cooking with it increases its health benefits.

1. On a cutting board with a chef's knife, peel the garlic. Using the garlic press, press the garlic and set it aside. Peel the onion. With a chef's knife, dice the onion and bell pepper. Cut the carrots into small rounds and set them aside.

2. Put a large pot on a burner on the stove and turn the heat to medium. Add the olive oil and heat it until hot but not smoking. Add the garlic, onion, and bell pepper to the pot and cook, stirring with a mixing spoon, until the onion is translucent (you can almost see through it).

3. Add the carrot rounds, the cumin, chili powder, salt, and pepper and stir for a minute. Add the chicken broth and stir to combine.

4. Put a colander in the sink. Open the cans of beans and tomatoes. Dump 2 cans of the black beans into the colander and rinse them with cold running water, moving them around a little bit with your hand until the water runs clear, and add them to the soup.

5. Increase the heat under the pot to high and cover with the lid. When the soup starts to boil, turn off the heat. At this point, you can add the can of tomatoes or, if you want a chunkier soup, you can wait until after you blend the soup. (I like to wait, but whatever you want to do works fine.)

6. Use an immersion blender to purée the soup right in the pot until smooth, or until no large chunks remain. (Or, if you need to use a regular blender, blend it in very small batches with the funnel cap

Ingredients

- 2 cloves garlic
- 1 medium onion
- 1 sweet bell pepper (any color)
- 3 carrots
- 2 tablespoons olive oil
- 2 teaspoons cumin
- 1 teaspoon chili powder
- ½ teaspoon salt
- ¼ teaspoon pepper
- 1 quart chicken broth or stock (canned or homemade, page 97)
- 3 (15-ounce) cans black beans
- 1 (15-ounce) can diced tomatoes

off to allow the steam to escape and to avoid burning yourself with exploding hot soup. Use a ladle to transfer a small amount of the soup to the blender and blend it until smooth, or until no large chunks remain. Transfer the puréed soup to another clean pot and continue to purée the soup in the same manner.)

7. Drain and rinse the remaining can of beans (see step 4).

8. Turn the heat under the soup pot back to high, then add the rinsed beans and, if you haven't already, the can of diced tomatoes. When the soup just starts to boil and everything is warmed through, the soup is ready to serve.

CREAMED CAULIFLOWER

By Paul

This is a great recipe to use as a substitute for mashed potatoes. Also, feel free to try different spices, but check with an adult before "going rogue."

ACTIVE TIME: 10–15 minutes > TOTAL TIME: 30–40 minutes > MAKES: about 5 servings

EQUIPMENT

Cutting board

Chef's knife

Steamer basket or colander

Medium pot with lid

Oven mitts

Fork

Colander (optional)

Measuring cups and spoons

Immersion blender or potato masher

Serving bowl or plates

INGREDIENTS

1 head of cauliflower

½ cup milk

½ cup shredded cheese (optional)

¼ cup cottage cheese

¼ cup sour cream (or yogurt)

1 teaspoon salt

½ teaspoon garlic powder

¼ teaspoon pepper

1. Wash the cauliflower. Using a cutting board and a chef's knife, cut it into small florets (small enough to blend with an immersion blender). Cut the large stem into smaller pieces too, but don't use the leaves.

2. Put a steamer basket into a medium pot, then add enough water to reach up to the steamer basket but not above it. If you don't have a steamer basket, put ½ inch of water into the pot.

3. Put the pot on a burner on the stove and turn the heat to high. When the water starts to boil, reduce the heat to low. Put the cauliflower pieces into the steamer basket (or directly into the water if you don't have a steamer basket), and put the lid on the pot. Steam the cauliflower for 10 minutes. Using oven mitts, take the lid off the pot and poke a piece of cauliflower with a fork. If the cauliflower is soft, it is done. If it isn't, put the lid back on for 5 minutes more.

4. When the cauliflower is soft, turn the heat off. Wearing oven mitts, lift the steamer basket out of the pot and pour the water into the sink, or put a colander in the sink and dump the cauliflower in it to drain (have an adult do this for you).

5. Transfer the cauliflower back into the pot. Add the milk, cheese, cottage cheese, sour cream, salt, garlic powder, and pepper.

6. If using an immersion blender blend the cauliflower mixture right in the pot until smooth. If you are using a potato masher, mash the mixture until it is uniform.

7. Transfer the creamed cauliflower to a serving bowl or individual plates. Serve warm or at room temperature as a side dish or as a main dish with toppings (see the box to the right).

TOPPING IDEAS

There are a ton of great toppings that go well with this recipe, including cheese, all sorts of veggies, chili, and whatever else you can think of (so basically whatever you would put on a baked potato and more)!

Egg Drop Soup

By Paul

Skill > Moderate

This recipe is super simple and, for sure, one of the quickest-to-make soup recipes ever. It makes a great lunch or starter for dinner.

ACTIVE TIME: 10 minutes > **TOTAL TIME: 25 minutes** > **MAKES: about 4 servings**

Equipment

Cutting board

Chef's knife

Whisk

Medium bowl

Medium pot

Measuring cups and spoons

Mixing spoon

Ingredients

2 green onions

4 eggs

1 quart chicken stock or broth (canned or homemade, page 97)

1 teaspoon salt

¼ teaspoon oregano

¼ teaspoon Italian seasoning

½ cup frozen peas

1. Using a cutting board and a chef's knife, cut off and discard the ends of the green onions and cut up the rest of the onions into small circular pieces. Set aside.

2. Using a whisk, whisk the eggs thoroughly in a medium bowl.

3. Put a medium pot on a burner on the stove and pour the broth into the pot. Stir in the salt, oregano, and Italian seasoning with a mixing spoon and turn the heat to high.

4. When the broth just comes to a boil, begin stirring the broth with the mixing spoon and slowly add the whisked eggs. (The stirring helps the eggs to cook in separate pieces.) The eggs will cook immediately. Turn the heat to low.

5. Add the green onions and peas and cook for 2 minutes more, until the peas are cooked through.

6. Serve immediately.

Egg Fried Rice

By Paul

Skill > Moderate

This recipe is kind of different from a lot of other recipes because you have to add the eggs in a weird way, and that's what makes it super fun to make! This recipe goes great with any Asian dish, especially a stir fry, but it's also great on its own!

ACTIVE TIME: 10–25 minutes (*depending on if you have already cooked rice*) > **TOTAL TIME: 25–40 minutes**
MAKES: 4–6 servings

Equipment

Cutting board

Chef's knife

Garlic press

Measuring cups and spoons

Medium pot with a lid

Mixing spoon

Ingredients

2 cloves garlic

1 small sweet bell pepper

¾ cup uncooked white rice or 2 cups leftover cooked white rice

2 tablespoons olive oil

½ teaspoon salt

¼ teaspoon black pepper

½ teaspoon dried crushed basil

½ teaspoon chili powder (optional)

3 eggs

1. Working on a cutting board with the chef's knife, peel the garlic. Crush the garlic with the garlic press. Using the chef's knife, cut enough of the bell pepper into small dice (cubes) to measure ½ cup and set the rest aside (use any leftovers for another recipe).

2. If you are using leftover cooked rice, skip to step 3 and start cooking the bell pepper in the oil without any rice in the pot (you will add the leftover rice later on in step 3). If you are making rice from scratch, put the uncooked rice in a medium pot with 1½ cups of water. Put the pot on a burner on the stove and turn the heat to high. When the rice mixture just comes to a boil, reduce the heat to low, put a lid on the pot, and cook the rice for 15 minutes. No peeking into the pot! After 15 minutes, remove the lid and push the rice to one side of the pot with a cooking spoon. Turn the heat off to allow the rice to cool a little.

3. Add the bell pepper and 1 tablespoon of the olive oil to the other side of the pot across from the newly cooked rice and turn the heat to medium. Make sure to keep the rice moving every once in a while so that it doesn't burn. When the bell pepper is almost cooked (limp), add the garlic and cook for about 30 seconds more, then add the salt, pepper, basil, and chili powder (if using) and stir until combined. If you are using leftover cooked rice, add it now and stir it into the bell pepper mixture, reheating it until hot.

– 78 –

4. Once everything is hot, push the rice mixture to the sides of the pot, leaving a hole in the middle. Pour the remaining 1 tablespoon olive oil into the hole.

5. Crack 1 egg into the hole. Break the yolk with your cooking spoon and stir it around in the hole a little bit. Add the remaining eggs, one at a time, and stir in the same manner. When all of the eggs are partially cooked, stir them around in the rice mixture until they are fully cooked. Turn off the heat and serve.

CHEESEBURGER CASSEROLE

By Anthony

Skill > Advanced

My five siblings and I can eat a lot of food, and casseroles are an easy way to feed us! Most kids love this one, because it combines many of the ingredients kids love best (parents like it, too).

ACTIVE TIME: 15 minutes > TOTAL TIME: 25 minutes > MAKES: 6–8 servings

EQUIPMENT

Large pot with a lid

Measuring cups and
    spoons

Colander

Oven mitts

9- by 13-inch baking dish

Cutting board

Chef's knife

Grater

Large skillet

Spatula or mixing spoon

Can opener

1. Fill a large pot three-quarters full with water and add 1 tablespoon of salt. Put the pot on a burner on the stove and turn the heat to high. Cover the pot with a lid and bring the water to a boil. When the water boils, remove the lid. Add the pasta to the pot and cook until just tender, according to the box instructions.

2. Put a colander in the sink. When the pasta is done, wearing oven mitts, carry the pot to the sink and drain the pasta in the colander (have an adult to do this for you). Set aside.

3. Preheat the oven to 375°F, and grease a 9- by-13-inch baking dish with a little bit of olive oil.

4. Working on a cutting board and using a chef's knife, peel the onion, cut it into very small pieces, and set aside. If using garlic cloves, peel and mince them and set aside. Using a grater, shred enough cheese to measure 3 cups and set aside.

5. Put a large skillet on a burner on the stove and turn the heat to medium-high. Add 1 tablespoon of olive oil to the skillet. When it is hot but not smoking, add the ground beef and cook, using a wooden spatula or spoon to chop it up into small pieces as it cooks.

6. When the meat is almost cooked through, add the onion powder and salt and pepper to taste, then add the onion pieces and cook for about 6 minutes, or until soft and slightly browned. Add the

– 80 –

INGREDIENTS

- 1 tablespoon salt, plus more for seasoning

- 2 cups pasta of choice (such as macaroni, rotini, and rotelle; gluten free works fine too)

- 1 tablespoon olive oil, plus more for greasing the baking dish

- 1 large onion

- 2 cloves garlic or ½ teaspoon garlic powder

- 3 cups cheese of choice (Cheddar is my favorite)

- 1 pound ground beef

- 1 tablespoon onion powder

- Freshly ground pepper, to taste

- 1 (28-ounce) can diced tomatoes

- 1 (6-ounce) can tomato paste

- Chopped pickles, pickle relish, chopped bacon, extra cheese, raw onions, mustard, or mayonnaise, for topping

garlic or garlic powder and cook, stirring, for 1 minute more. Using the can opener, open the canned tomatoes and the tomato paste, add them to the skillet, and stir to combine. Reduce the heat to low heat and cook, stirring for another few minutes, until everything is warmed through and combined well.

7. Pour the beef mixture into the prepared baking dish (ask a grownup for help if it is too heavy). Add the pasta and stir until combined well. Sprinkle the shredded cheese over the casserole.

8. Put the casserole in the oven and cook for 10 minutes, or until the cheese is melted. Serve immediately with the toppings of your choice.

TACO CASSEROLE

By Anthony

Skill > Advanced

Every Tuesday is Taco Tuesday at our house, and this casserole version of tacos is our go-to recipe. There are so many ways to mix it up and top it with things like salsa, sour cream, or anything else you like.

ACTIVE TIME: 25 minutes > TOTAL TIME: 35 minutes > MAKES: 6–8 servings

EQUIPMENT

Large skillet

Spatula

Cutting board

Chef's knife

Measuring cups and
    spoons

9- by 13-inch glass baking
    dish

Can opener

Oven mitts

Tip

**If there are leftovers,
try scrambling
them with eggs and
rolling the mixture
in tortillas to make
breakfast tacos.**

1. Preheat the oven to 375°F.

2. Put a large skillet on a burner on the stove and turn the heat to medium-high. Add the ground beef and cook, stirring and chopping it up into small pieces with a spatula until it is brown and no pink remains.

3. Meanwhile, working on a cutting board and using a chef's knife, peel the red onion, chop it into small pieces, and set aside. Cut off the ends of the green onions and thinly slice the remainder into rounds. Set aside.

4. When the ground beef is cooked through, add the chili powder, cumin, onion powder, garlic powder, salt, and pepper and stir to combine. Add the chopped red onion and cook the mixture 5 minutes more, or until the onion is soft.

5. When the onion is soft, spoon the meat mixture into a 9- by 13-inch baking dish.

6. Using a can opener, open and drain the beans, if necessary. Transfer to a clean skillet. Put the skillet on a burner on the stove and turn the heat to medium-high. Cook the beans, stirring, until warmed through. Turn off the heat and move the skillet to a cool burner. Add 1 cup of the shredded cheese and the salsa to the beans and stir to combine, then spoon over the meat mixture in the baking dish.

Ingredients

- 1 pound ground beef
- 1 red onion
- 2 green onions
- 1 tablespoon chili powder (not too spicy hot)
- 1 tablespoon cumin
- 1 teaspoon onion powder
- ½ teaspoon garlic powder
- ½ teaspoon salt
- ½ teaspoon pepper
- 1 (15-ounce) can refried beans or black beans
- 3 cups shredded cheese
- 1 cup salsa
- 1–2 tomatoes
- Corn chips and sour cream, for serving

Sprinkle the remaining 2 cups of cheese over the meat and beans. Now sprinkle the sliced green onions on top of the casserole.

7. Wearing oven mitts, transfer the casserole to the hot oven and bake for 8 minutes, or until the cheese is melted.

8. Wearing oven mitts, remove the casserole from the oven and put on a cool burner on the stove. Let cool 5 minutes.

9. While the casserole is cooling, using a cutting board and a chef's knife, chop the tomato into small pieces (you should have about 1 cup).

10. Sprinkle the tomato over the top of the casserole. Serve over corn chips and top with sour cream, if desired.

Tomato, Zucchini, & Mozzarella Bake

 By Katie

Skill > Advanced

A few years ago, zucchini took over my family's garden. It was everywhere, so we made it into pasta, shredded it into cheesy egg muffins, and even turned it into pizza. Of all the ways we prepared it, this is one of my favorites.

ACTIVE TIME: 10 minutes > TOTAL TIME: 35–40 minutes > MAKES: 5 servings

Equipment

Cutting board
Chef's knife
Large bowl
Measuring cups and spoons
2 large mixing spoons
9- by- 13-inch baking dish
Oven mitts
Fork
Cooling rack

Ingredients

3 large zucchini
4 garlic cloves, minced
1½ cups cherry tomatoes
½ cup shredded mozzarella cheese or dairy-free mozzarella cheese
1½ teaspoons dried basil
2 teaspoons avocado or olive oil
¾ teaspoon salt
⅛ teaspoon black pepper

1. Preheat the oven to 350°F.

2. Working on a cutting board and using a chef's knife, cut the zucchini into ½-inch thick slices, cut each slice into four pieces, then transfer to a large bowl. Peel and mince the garlic, then add it to the bowl. Add the tomatoes, cheese, basil, oil, salt, and pepper to the bowl and toss with two large spoons until combined. Transfer to a 9- by- 13-inch baking dish.

3. Wearing oven mitts, place the dish in the hot oven and bake for 25–30 minutes, or until the zucchini is tender when pierced with a fork.

4. Wearing oven mitts, remove the baking dish from the oven and transfer to a cooling rack. Serve warm.

MARGHERITA PIZZA

BY Paul

Skill > Moderate

As I was editing one of my mom's interviews with a chef, I watched him demonstrate how to make Margherita pizza, and for months, I wanted to try it. Now I can make this cool recipe my own and share it with you in this cookbook!

ACTIVE TIME: 40–60 minutes > TOTAL TIME: 55–75 minutes > MAKES: 8 individual pizzas

EQUIPMENT

Kitchen mixer with a dough hook attachment (or a mixing bowl or spoon) (optional)

Measuring cups and spoons

A couple of spoons

Whisk

Plate

Flexible cutting board

2 baking sheets or baking stones

Rolling pin

Chef's knife or serrated knife

Oven mitts

(Ingredients list is on the following page)

1. To make the crust: Add the water, yeast, and sugar to the bowl of a kitchen mixer with a dough hook attachment. If you don't have one, use a regular mixing bowl.

2. Whisk the ingredients until the mixture looks uniform. When bubbles appear at the top of the bowl, set it aside for about 8 minutes.

3. Add 1 tablespoon of the olive oil and the salt to the yeast mixture and whisk until the consistency is uniform. Set the kitchen mixer with the dough hook attached to low, turn it on, and slowly pour in the flour 1 cup at a time.

4. After all of the flour is incorporated, the dough should start to pull away from the sides.

5. Reset the mixer to medium and run it for about 5 minutes to knead the dough. (If you don't have a mixer, knead the dough by hand.) When the dough is ready, use the remaining 1 tablespoon of olive oil to coat it, then roll it around a bit with your hands. Form the dough into a ball.

6. Cover the mixing bowl with a plate and let the dough rise for 30 minutes.

7. While the dough is rising, preheat the oven to 450°F.

(continued)

Ingredients

CRUST

1 cup warm water (about body temperature)

2¼ teaspoons active dry yeast, or use one ½-ounce packet

1 teaspoon sugar

About 2 tablespoons olive oil

1½ teaspoons salt

3 cups white whole wheat flour

TOPPINGS

1–2 tomatoes, sliced (1 heirloom or two Roma)

3–4 cups pizza or pasta sauce from a jar

2–5 ounces fresh mozzarella cheese

½ cup fresh basil leaves

2 tablespoons grated Parmesan cheese

1–2 tablespoons olive oil

Salt to taste

8. Dust a flexible cutting board with flour. When the dough has risen to double its original size, remove it from the mixing bowl and place it on the dusted cutting board. Tear it into 8 pieces. Roll the pieces into balls and use a rolling pin to roll out the dough into thin circles, about 5 inches in diameter.

9. Once all the dough has been rolled out, place the circles on two baking sheets or baking stones and bake them in the oven for 7 minutes.

10. While the crusts are baking, prepare the toppings by using a chef's knife or serrated knife to slice the tomatoes.

11. When the crusts are done, using oven mitts, remove them from the oven and add the sauce, spreading it out thinly to the edge of the circles. Add the tomato slices, 1–3 per pizza, depending on how wide the slices are. Scoop out small chunks of mozzarella with a spoon and add 4–7 pieces to each pizza. Remember, Margherita pizza isn't supposed to be totally covered in cheese, and the cheese will expand when it melts, so don't overdo it.

12. Put the pizzas back in the oven for another 7–8 minutes.

13. Using oven mitts, remove the pizzas, and add the basil immediately so that the leaves wilt on the hot pizza. Sprinkle the Parmesan cheese and drizzle the olive oil over the pizzas. Add salt to taste, if you like, and serve the pizza hot or cold.

Chicken Ranch Wraps with Greek Yogurt Ranch Dressing

By Anthony

Skill > Easy

These chicken wraps are really easy to make and are a great lunch to take to school.

ACTIVE TIME: 10 minutes > TOTAL TIME: 10 minutes > SERVES: 4

Equipment

Bowl

Plates

Griddle (optional)

Whisk

Ingredients

2 cups leftover cooked chicken (or store-bought rotisserie chicken), cubed

1 cup grated cheese

1 head romaine lettuce, finely shredded

1 tomato, sliced (optional)

Ranch dressing to taste (see Greek Yogurt Ranch Dressing, below)

Tortillas, heated on a dry hot griddle or skillet

1. Place all the ingredients in a bowl, except for the tortillas.

2. Place the tortillas on individual serving plates.

3. Layer ½ cup shredded chicken, ¼ cup cheese, some shredded lettuce, and a slice of tomato onto each tortilla. Drizzle ranch dressing, to taste, over the top.

4. Roll up the wraps and serve them immediately.

NOTE: *You can warm up tortillas on a dry griddle or skillet over low to medium heat on the stove—3–4 minutes on each side—or in a panini press.*

GREEK YOGURT RANCH DRESSING

MAKES A LITTLE OVER 1 CUP

1 cup plain full-fat
  Greek yogurt

1 teaspoon onion salt (or
  ½ salt plus 1 teaspoon
  onion powder)

1 teaspoon garlic powder

2 teaspoons dried parsley

½ teaspoon dried dill

½ teaspoon black pepper

— In a bowl, whisk together the yogurt, onion salt, garlic powder, dried parsley, dried dill, and black peper. Add up to ¼ cup of water, if needed, to thin the dressing. Enjoy as a dip or dressing.

Baked Fish Sticks with Tartar Sauce

By Anthony

Skill > Advanced

Fish sticks are a classic kids' favorite. I hope you like my version of them!

ACTIVE TIME: 30 minutes > TOTAL TIME: 30 minutes > SERVES: 4

Equipment

2 large plates

Medium-size bowl

Whisk

Cutting board

Chef's knife

Large baking sheet

Oven mitts

Spatula

Small bowl

Jar

PAN FRY OPTION

After step 7, place some olive oil in a large pan and fry the fish over medium-high heat until it's golden brown and flaky on the inside.

1. Preheat the oven to 400°F.

2. Place the flour on a plate.

3. In a bowl, whisk the eggs, and then whisk in the salt, pepper, onion powder, and garlic powder.

4. On another plate, place the panko breadcrumbs (gluten-free panko breadcrumbs or crushed crackers).

5. Using a cutting board and chef's knife, carefully cut the cod into ¾-inch pieces.

6. Dredge each piece of the fish in the flour. Next, dip the fish into the whisked eggs, and then press each piece of the fish into the breadcrumbs until they're evenly coated.

7. Drizzle a baking sheet with olive oil and gently place the fish sticks on it.

8. Bake the fish sticks for 5 minutes.

9. After 5 minutes, using oven mitts, remove the baking sheet from the oven. Flip the fish with a spatula, drizzle a little of the olive oil over the top, and bake another 8–9 minutes. Dip in tartar sauce, if you like. Enjoy!

Ingredients

- 1 cup all-purpose flour (or substitute gluten-free flour)
- 2 large eggs, beaten
- 1 teaspoon salt
- ½ teaspoon freshly ground black pepper
- 1 tablespoon onion powder
- 1 teaspoon garlic powder
- 1 cup panko breadcrumbs (or gluten-free panko breadcrumbs or crushed crackers)
- 1 cup seasoned, dry, organic breadcrumbs (or use crushed crackers)
- 1 pound cod fillets
- Olive oil for greasing the pan and drizzling over the fish

TARTAR SAUCE

MAKES A LITTLE OVER 1 CUP

- 1 cup mayonnaise
- ¼ cup dill pickle relish or finely chopped dill pickles
- 1 tablespoon lemon juice
- 1 teaspoon Dijon mustard

— In a small bowl, mix the mayonnaise, dill pickle, lemon juice, and mustard together. Remove to a jar and refrigerate for at 2 hours or overnight before serving.

Best Burger with Secret Yum Sauce

By Anthony

Skill > Advanced

Everyone loves burgers and you can make delicious ones in your kitchen with this recipe. Secret Yum Sauce gives it extra flavor and a special twist.

ACTIVE TIME: 30 minutes > TOTAL TIME: 30 minutes > SERVES: 4

EQUIPMENT

Skillet

Spatula

Heatproof plates

Oven mitts

Small bowl

INGREDIENTS

24 ounces ground chuck
(6 ounces per burger)

1 teaspoon salt

1 teaspoon pepper

1 teaspoon onion powder

4–6 buns (or use lettuce,
such as Romaine, for
bun-free burgers)

2 tablespoons butter

Sliced cheese, optional

Lettuce, tomato, and
onion (optional)

1. Divide the meat into 4 balls (or 6 balls, if you want smaller burgers). Use the palm of your hand to press down on each of the balls to form a patty. Press both thumbs gently into the middle of each patty to make a small indention. This helps keep the burger flat while it cooks.

2. Sprinkle the burgers with the salt, pepper, and onion powder.

3. Open the buns, if you are using them, and spread butter on each side with a butter knife. Heat a skillet over medium-high heat.

4. Place the buns, two at a time, open side down, in the skillet and toast for 2–3 minutes or until the bread is golden brown and slightly crispy. Remove the skillet from the stovetop and, using a spatula, transfer the buns to a heatproof plate. Put the plate in a warm oven to keep the buns from getting cold.

5. Place the burgers in the skillet (two at a time, if there isn't enough room to cook all of them at once) and cook them for about 4 minutes on each side over medium-high heat. Flip the burgers when the edges start to turn brown and juices build up in the indentations you've made. Flip and cook the other side of the burgers for about 4 more minutes. Add a slice of cheese to each of the burgers, if you like, until it is just melted. Using oven mitts,

take the skillet off the heat and let the burgers sit for about 5 minutes while you make Secret Yum Sauce (see the recipe below).

6. Serve each burger on a bun with Secret Yum Sauce and other toppings like onions, tomatoes, and lettuce. (My family also loves adding bacon!)

SECRET YUM SAUCE

MAKES ABOUT 2 CUPS

½ cup mayonnaise

¼ cup ketchup

¼ cup pickle relish

— Place the mayonnaise, ketchup, and pickle relish in a small bowl and stir to combine.

Dinner

Fried Broccoli & Cauliflower >>> 96

Chicken Broth >>> 97

Maple-Glazed Chicken Thighs >>> 98

Super-Quick Gravy >>> 99

Simple Mashed Potatoes >>> 100

Caramel Carrots >>> 101

Turkey Chili >>> 102

Pizza Cauliflower Soup >>> 104

Cheeseburger Soup >>> 106

Garden-Fresh Pesto Pasta >>> 109

Great-Grandma's Spaghetti from Italy >>> 111

Kid-Friendly Broccoli >>> 113

Grilled Cheese >>> 114

Pinto Gallo (Gallo Pinto) >>> 116

Crispy, Crunchy Potatoes >>> 119

Oven-Roasted Green Beans >>> 121

Oven-Baked Sweet Potato Fries >>> 123

Coconut Chicken Nuggets >>> 124

Lime-Marinated Steak >>> 126

Fish Tacos >>> 128

Mediterranean Sun-Dried Tomato Chicken >>> 131

Honey-Mustard Chicken >>> 132

Cheesy Beef, Potato, & Carrot Casserole >>> 133

FRIED BROCCOLI & CAULIFLOWER

By Abigail

Skill > Moderate

Some kids hate broccoli and cauliflower. I guess you could say my parents did a good job, because when I was a little kid, they were my favorite vegetables. Mom called them little trees. Then one day, she started frying them up and making them crispy. After that, I completely forgot about eating them raw.

ACTIVE TIME: 30 minutes > TOTAL TIME: 30 minutes > MAKES: 5 servings

EQUIPMENT

Cutting board

Chef's knife

Measuring cups and spoons

Large skillet

Mixing spoon or spatula

INGREDIENTS

About 1 large head broccoli (4 cups chopped)

About 1 small head cauliflower (4 cups chopped)

2 tablespoons olive oil

1. Working on a cutting board and using a chef's knife, chop up the broccoli into large pieces, then chop up the cauliflower into large pieces (you will need about 4 cups of each).

2. Put a large skillet on a burner on the stove and turn the heat to medium. When the skillet is hot, pour the olive oil in the pan along with the broccoli and cauliflower pieces. Cook the vegetables, stirring only every 2–4 minutes, until crispy. (Do not constantly stir; allowing the veggies to sit in the pan without being moved will make them nice and crispy). When the vegetables are just cooked through and crispy, remove the skillet from the heat and turn the burner off.

3. Serve immediately.

SERVING IDEA

Serve these veggies with meat, Garden-Fresh Pesto Pasta (page 109), or another family favorite main dish. Our family also likes this alongside rice or soup.

CHICKEN BROTH

By Abigail

Nothing is better than warm, salty, soothing chicken broth. I remember all those sick days at home holding a warm mug of magical broth in my hand, snuggling up to my daddy and laughing.

ACTIVE TIME: 20 minutes > TOTAL TIME: 8 hours and 20 minutes > MAKES: 4 servings

EQUIPMENT

Large pot with a lid
Cutting board
Chef's knife
Measuring spoons
Mixing spoon
Oven mitts
Strainer
Storage bags and
  containers, if freezing

INGREDIENTS

2 pounds chicken bones
1 onion (chilled in the
  fridge)
2 carrots
2 cloves garlic
2 tablespoons apple cider
  vinegar
1½ tablespoons sea salt

1. Put the chicken bones in a large pot.

2. Working on a cutting board and using a chef's knife, peel and cut the chilled onion (putting it in the fridge will keep your eyes from tearing as much) into small pieces and add them to the pot. Chop the carrots into small pieces and add them to the pot. Peel and mince the garlic cloves and add them to the pot, too.

3. Add the apple cider vinegar and sea salt to the pot and stir together with a mixing spoon.

4. Put the pot in the sink and add enough water to the pot to cover the bones fully, by 2 inches.

5. Put the pot on a burner on the stove and turn the heat to high. Bring the mixture to a boil, then turn down the heat to low and put the lid on the pot. The broth needs to simmer for 8 hours for all the flavors to blend.

6. When the broth is done, turn off the stove. Using oven mitts, carefully move the pot to a cool burner. Remove the lid from the pan and let it cool completely.

7. Strain the broth from the bones and veggies.

8. Serve the broth on its own or use it to make other recipes, like soup or gravy.

MAPLE-GLAZED CHICKEN THIGHS

By Anthony

**Skill > Moderate

This chicken tastes fancy but is really easy to make. The mixture of maple syrup and soy sauce or coconut aminos makes a great sweet and salty sauce.

ACTIVE TIME: 5 minutes > TOTAL TIME: 35 minutes > MAKES: 4–6 servings

EQUIPMENT

Medium bowl

Measuring cups and spoons

Whisk or spoon

Plastic wrap

9- by 13-inch baking dish

Oven mitts

Instant-read thermometer

INGREDIENTS

⅓ cup maple syrup

¼ cup coconut aminos or soy sauce

1 teaspoon onion powder

½ teaspoon garlic powder

Salt, to taste

Pepper, to taste

8 boneless, skinless chicken thighs

2 tablespoons olive oil

1. In a large bowl, add the maple syrup, coconut aminos or soy sauce, onion powder, garlic powder, salt, and pepper, and whisk or stir to combine. Add the chicken thighs to the bowl and, using your hands, turn the thighs over in the marinade until it is well coated. **Wash your hands and cooking space throughly to avoid spreading bacteria.** Cover the bowl with plastic wrap and transfer to the refrigerator to chill overnight or up to 24 hours.

2. Preheat the oven to 425°F and drizzle the olive oil in the bottom of a 9- by 13-inch baking dish.

3. Place the chicken thighs in the dish, leaving as much space as possible between them, and pour any remaining marinade over the chicken.

4. Place the baking dish in the hot oven and bake the chicken for 30 minutes, or until cooked through and well browned. (To test for doneness, using oven mitts, transfer the baking dish to a cool burner on the top of the stove and insert an instant-read thermometer into a chicken thigh. It should read at least 165°F. If the temperature is lower, return the chicken to the oven and cook it for 5 minutes more before checking again.)

Super-Quick Gravy

By Anthony

Skill > Moderate

Everyone should have a great gravy recipe! Gravy can be used to top anything from a turkey at Thanksgiving to biscuits for breakfast, but my favorite way to use it is to make poutine. If you haven't heard of poutine, you make it by topping fries (see Oven-Baked Sweet Potato Fries, page 123) with gravy and some cheese curds. FYI, poutine was named the tenth greatest Canadian invention of all time, beating out the electron microscope, the BlackBerry, and even the paint roller!

ACTIVE TIME: 15–20 minutes > TOTAL TIME: 15–20 minute > MAKES: 4–6 servings

Equipment

Medium saucepan

Butter knife

Measuring cups and spoons

Whisk

Ingredients

2 cups chicken broth (preferably homemade, see page 97, or canned)

4 tablespoons butter

¼ cup flour (organic or gluten-free)

½ teaspoon salt

½ teaspoon pepper

2 teaspoons onion powder

½ teaspoon garlic powder

1. If you are making your own chicken broth (it really makes a difference to make the real thing, so I hope you do it), make it at least 1 day ahead and store it in the refrigerator.

2. Put a medium saucepan on a burner on the stove, and with a butter knife transfer the butter to the pan. Turn the heat to medium and melt the butter (do not let it brown).

3. Using a whisk, whisk the flour into the butter, making sure to get rid of all the lumps.

4. Add the salt, pepper, onion powder, and garlic powder and whisk to blend thoroughly. Continue to whisk and cook the flour mixture for 3–4 minutes, just until it turns light brown.

5. Turn down the heat to low. Slowly add the chicken broth, a little at a time, whisking constantly, until all of it is added.

6. Turn up the heat to medium and continue to cook the gravy for another few minutes, whisking constantly, until thickened.

SIMPLE MASHED POTATOES

 Will

Skill > Moderate

Topped with butter and salt, this is one of the most delicious recipes you will ever make.

ACTIVE TIME: 20 minutes > TOTAL TIME: 45 minutes > MAKES: 8 servings

EQUIPMENT

Vegetable peeler

Cutting board

Chef's knife

Large pot with a lid

Measuring cups and
  spoons

Fork

Colander

Oven mitts

Potato masher

Large mixing spoon or
  rubber scraper

Handheld electric mixer

INGREDIENTS

10 large potatoes

1 tablespoon coarse
  sea salt

1 pound butter

About 3 cups cream

Ground black pepper and
  sea salt, to taste

1. Using a vegetable peeler, peel the potatoes. Working on a cutting board and using a chef's knife, cut the potatoes into 2-inch pieces. Transfer them to a large pot.

2. Transfer the pot to the sink and cover the potatoes by 2 inches with cold water. Add 1 tablespoon of the sea salt to the pot.

3. Put the pot on a burner on the stove and turn the heat to high. Put the lid on the pot and bring the water to a boil. Boil the potatoes for 20–25 minutes, or until they are soft enough to be easily pierced with a fork.

4. Put a large colander in the sink. Wearing oven mitts, carefully transfer the pot to the sink and drain the potatoes in the colander (have an adult do this for you). Dump the potatoes back into the pot and transfer the pot to a cool burner on the stove.

5. Using a potato masher, immediately mash the potatoes in the pot. Add the butter and stir the mashed potatoes with a large mixing spoon or spatula until the butter is melted and no lumps remain. Add the cream a little at a time, stirring constantly, until the desired consistency is reached.

6. Using a handheld electric mixer, whip the potatoes right in the pot until smooth and fluffy. Season to taste with freshly ground black pepper and sea salt.

CARAMEL CARROTS

By Abigail

Is there something you used to always beg your mom or dad to cook for you? For me, it was Caramel Carrots. I would've eaten the entire pot if my mom hadn't stopped me. Now I can make this amazing side dish on my own.

ACTIVE TIME: 10 minutes **>** **TOTAL TIME:** 30 minutes **>** **MAKES:** 4 servings

EQUIPMENT

Cutting board
Chef's knife
Small pot
Measuring cups
Mixing spoon

INGREDIENTS

5 medium or 3 large carrots
4 tablespoons butter
2 tablespoons honey

1. Working on a cutting board and using a chef's knife, cut the carrots into bite-size rounds. Dump the carrot rounds into a small pot and add the butter and honey.

2. Put the pot on a burner on the stove and turn the heat to high. Put the lid on the pot and cook the carrots for 3 minutes, or until it just starts to boil. (After 3 minutes, remove the lid from the pot to see if the mixture is boiling. If not, put the lid back on and wait for 30 seconds or so.) When the mixture comes to a boil, stir the carrots with a wooden spoon for about 20 seconds or so, then put the lid back on. Reduce the heat to medium heat and cook the carrots, undisturbed, for 5 minutes more.

3. After 5 minutes, remove the lid and stir again. Do this every 5 minutes until the carrots are easy to break with the mixing spoon. Turn off the burner and move the pot to a cool burner.

4. Serve the carrots, topping each serving with some crystallized honey from the pot.

NOTE *Immediately after removing the carrots, be sure to soak the pot in the sink with some hot soapy water to keep the honey from sticking to the pot. After dinner, the pot will be much easier to clean.*

TURKEY CHILI

By Katie

When I first made this recipe, my little brother ate four bowls of it in one day. Luckily, you can easily double the recipe to have plenty on hand for another meal!

ACTIVE TIME: 25 minutes > TOTAL TIME: 45–50 minutes > MAKES: 4 servings

EQUIPMENT

Cutting board

Chef's knife

Measuring cups and
  spoons

Little bowl

Large pot

Mixing spoon or spatula

1. Working on a cutting board and using a chef's knife, peel and chop the onion into small pieces. Peel and mince the garlic. Set aside.

2. Add the chili powder, cumin, coriander, pepper, and oregano to a little bowl and set aside.

3. Put a large pot on a burner on the stove. Add the oil to the pot and turn the heat to medium. When the oil is hot but not smoking, add the onions and garlic to the pot and cook for about 5 minutes, stirring occasionally with a mixing spoon or spatula, until the onions are lightly browned.

4. Add the ground turkey to the pot and continue to cook for 5 minutes more, breaking up the turkey with the spatula into small, bite-size pieces.

5. Add the tomatoes, the spices you set aside, and the chicken broth or water, and increase the heat to high. Bring the chili to a boil, then reduce the heat to low, cover the pot with a lid, and simmer for 25 minutes.

6. Sprinkle the arrowroot powder over the top of the chili, stir it in thoroughly with the spatula, then simmer for 5 minutes more until thickened slightly. Season the chili with salt to taste. Turn off the burner and transfer the pot to a cool burner.

7. Serve the chili in bowls topped with your favorite toppings.

Ingredients

- 1 large onion
- 2 cloves garlic
- 2 tablespoons chili powder
- 1½ teaspoons cumin
- ½ teaspoon coriander
- 1 teaspoon ground black pepper
- ¼ teaspoon dried oregano
- 1 tablespoon coconut oil or avocado oil
- 1 pound ground turkey
- 12 ounces peeled diced tomatoes (1½ cups)
- ⅓ cup chicken broth (page 97) or water
- Salt to taste
- 1½ teaspoons arrowroot powder
- Toppings (optional): grated cheese, chopped avocado, chopped green onions

PIZZA CAULIFLOWER SOUP

By Paul

Skill > Moderate

I really liked the cauliflower soup that my mom made, but I felt it lacked something, so I decided to make it into a pizza soup! Different spices can make a recipe taste way different.

ACTIVE TIME: 25–30 minutes > TOTAL TIME: 35–45 minutes > MAKES: about 6 servings

EQUIPMENT

Cutting board

Chef's knife

Bowls for the cut
    vegetables

Garlic press

Large pot with a lid

Measuring cups and
    spoons

Mixing spoon

Can opener

Fork

Immersion blender
    or regular blender

1. Working on a cutting board and using a chef's knife, prepare the vegetables. Peel the onion, dice it, and set it aside. Chop the cauliflower into medium-size florets and set aside. Cut the potatoes into small pieces and set aside. Peel the garlic, crush it in the garlic press, and set it aside.

2. Put a large pot on a burner on the stove and turn the heat to medium. Add the olive oil and let it heat for 1–2 minutes. Add the onion and garlic and cook, stirring with a mixing spoon, until the onion is soft.

3. Open the cans of tomatoes with the can opener. Add the cauliflower, potatoes, broth, tomatoes, oregano, Italian seasoning, ground fennel, and salt, and stir to combine. Make sure the broth covers everything. If it doesn't, add enough water to cover everything. Increase the heat to high, cover the pot with the lid, and bring the mixture to a boil. When the mixture starts to boil, reduce the heat to low and simmer the soup for 10 minutes, or until the cauliflower and potatoes are soft.

4. Check the cauliflower and potatoes by piercing them with a fork. If they are soft, turn the heat off. If not, simmer the soup for a few more minutes.

5. Using an immersion blender, purée the soup right in the pot (see the safety tip on the next page) until it is smooth. (Alternatively, use a regular blender to purée the soup. Just remember that you must blend the soup in very small batches with the funnel cap off to allow

INGREDIENTS

1 medium onion

1 medium cauliflower
head (about 6 cups
medium-size florets)

2 large or 3 small potatoes
or turnips (about
5 cups diced, peeled
or unpeeled)

6 garlic cloves

2 tablespoons olive oil

8 cups chicken or beef
broth or stock

1 (15-ounce) can diced
tomatoes

2 teaspoons dried oregano

1 teaspoon Italian
seasoning

1 teaspoon ground fennel

Salt to taste

2 cups shredded
mozzarella cheese

the steam to escape and to avoid burning yourself with exploding hot soup. Use a ladle to transfer a small amount of the soup to the blender and blend it until smooth. Transfer the puréed soup to another clean pot and continue to purée the soup in the same manner until all of the soup is smooth.)

6. Add the cheese, stir it in until it is almost melted, and serve the soup.

Safety Tip

When using an immersion blender to purée the soup, make sure the blade of the blender is completely under the surface, otherwise it will splash hot liquid all over you. Also, don't tilt the blender, because that will also cause it to splash.

CHEESEBURGER SOUP

By Paul

Skill > Moderate

This is arguably my family's favorite soup recipe! Just about everyone in the family can help out with some part of it.

ACTIVE TIME: 40–50 minutes > TOTAL TIME: 55–65 minutes > MAKES: 4–8 servings

EQUIPMENT

Cutting board

Chef's knife

Large pot with lid

Cooking spoon

Measuring cups and spoons

Can opener

Fork

1. Working on a cutting board and using a chef's knife, prepare the vegetables. Crush the garlic with the side of the knife, peel it, then mince it and set it aside. Peel the onion, dice it and the potatoes, and set them aside. Cut the carrots into small rounds and set them aside also.

2. Put a large pot on a burner on the stove and turn the heat to medium. Add the ground beef and cook, breaking it up into small pieces with a cooking spoon until it turns brown with no pink remaining.

3. Add the onions to the beef and cook, stirring, it until soft.

4. Add the garlic, potatoes, carrots, salt, and pepper and cook, stirring everything together, for a few minutes more.

5. Using the can opener, open the cans of kidney beans and tomatoes. Add the kidney beans, tomato sauce, and broth and stir to combine. Increase the heat to high, and put the lid on the pot. Bring the mixture to a boil, then reduce the heat to low and simmer for 15 minutes, or until the carrots and potatoes are soft.

6. Check the carrots and potatoes by piercing them with a fork. If they are soft, turn off the heat. If not, cook the mixture, covered, for about 5 minutes more and check again.

7. Add the cheese, stir it in until melted, and serve the soup.

INGREDIENTS

3 cloves garlic

1 large or 2 small onions

6 medium or 8–9 small potatoes (peeled or unpeeled)

5 carrots (any size is fine)

1 pound ground beef

Salt, to taste

⅛ teaspoon pepper

1 (15-ounce) can kidney beans, rinsed and drained

1 cup tomato sauce (half of a 15-ounce can)

8 cups broth or stock (chicken or beef)

1 cup grated Cheddar cheese, mild or sharp, plus more if you'd like

GREAT ADDITIONS

I like to stir diced dill pickles and some pickle juice into my bowl of cheeseburger soup. Or, I stir in a bit of sour cream for a bit of tang. Best of all is *bacon*! Just cook up a few pieces of bacon and then, when it's cool enough to handle, break it up into small pieces and sprinkle it on top of your soup.

Garden-Fresh Pesto Pasta

By Abigail

I absolutely *adore* pesto. Whenever I see pesto at the store, I beg my mom to get it. Whenever I get to make dinner, my thoughts immediately go to pesto. So, here is my take on this magical food.

ACTIVE TIME: 30 minutes > TOTAL TIME: 30 minutes > MAKES: 4 servings

Equipment

Large pot

Measuring cups and spoons

Food processor

Cutting board

Paring knife

Rubber spatula

Colander

Oven mitts

Large serving bowl

Ingredients

1 tablespoon salt, plus more for seasoning

3 cups gluten-free or regular pasta (uncooked)

2 cloves garlic

2 cups fresh basil leaves (packed down)

¼ cup pine nuts or walnuts

⅔ cups extra virgin olive oil

½ cup grated Parmesan cheese, plus more for serving

Freshly ground pepper, to taste

1. Put a large pot in the sink and fill the pot three-fourths full with cold water. Add 1 tablespoon of salt to the water. Put the pot on a burner on the stove and turn the heat to high. Bring the water to a boil. Add the pasta and cook until tender, according to the package directions.

2. Meanwhile, put the food processor on the counter. Using a cutting board and paring knife, peel the garlic. Add the garlic, basil, and pine nuts or walnuts, put the top on firmly, and blend until a thick paste forms. If the paste gets stuck on the sides of the bowl, turn off the food processor and use a rubber spatula to scrape it into the bottom of the bowl; then continue to blend.

3. Add the oil and Parmesan cheese to the paste and blend it for 5 seconds more, until it's combined. Set aside.

4. Put a large colander in the sink. When the pasta is ready, wearing oven mitts, take the hot pot to the sink and drain the pasta in the colander (have an adult do this for you).

5. Dump the drained pasta into a large serving bowl. Add all the pesto to the cooked pasta and stir it together until well combined.

6. Top the pasta with some extra Parmesan cheese and salt and pepper to taste and serve.

MAKE THIS AHEAD

The sauce gets better with age, so this recipe is great on the second, third, and even fourth day after you make it. Also, for a great lunch, the meatballs can be served on some toast for a meatball sub.

Great-Grandma's Spaghetti from Italy

By Anthony

Skill > Moderate

Part of my dad's family came from Sicily, so this recipe is a big part of our family tradition, even though the marinara (tomato) sauce probably originated in Naples, and the idea of spaghetti and meatballs only became popular in the United States when struggling Italian immigrants discovered they could make the meatballs with cheap cuts of meat and stale bread.

ACTIVE TIME: 40 minutes > TOTAL TIME: 40 minutes > MAKES: 6–8 servings

Equipment

Large bowl

Measuring cups and spoons

Plates, one for refrigerating and one for testing doneness

Cutting board

Chef's knife

Large skillet with a lid

Wooden spoon

Fork

Can opener

2 large pots

Mixing spoon

Oven mitts

Colander

(Ingredients list is on the following page)

1. In a large bowl, add the beef, turkey, bread crumbs, onion powder, Italian seasoning, garlic powder, and Parmesan cheese. Using clean hands, gently mix everything together until it combined well (but don't pack it down), then form balls about 1½ inches in diameter. Once all the meatballs are formed, transfer the plate to the refrigerator. Wash your hands throughly.

2. Working on a cutting board and using a chef's knife, peel the onion and cut it into ½-inch pieces. Put a large skillet on a burner on the stove. Pour the olive oil into the skillet and turn the burner to medium heat. When the oil is hot but not smoking, add the onion and stir with a wooden spoon to coat the onion with the oil.

3. Place the meatballs in a single layer in the onion mixture in the skillet and cover the skillet with a lid. Every 3–4 minutes, remove the lid and stir the meatballs and onions. After about 6–8 minutes, keep the lid off and continue to cook, stirring the meatballs and onions until they are cooked through, about 12–15 minutes more. If the onions are browning too quickly, reduce the heat just a little.

(continued)

INGREDIENTS

FOR THE MEATBALLS AND ONION

1 pound ground beef

1 pound ground turkey

1 cup bread crumbs

1 tablespoon onion powder

1 tablespoon Italian seasoning

1 teaspoon garlic powder

½ cup Parmesan cheese

1 large yellow onion

¼ cup olive oil

FOR THE SAUCE

1 (28-ounce) can tomato sauce

1 (28-ounce) can crushed or diced tomatoes

1 (6-ounce) can tomato paste

2 tablespoons Italian seasoning

1 tablespoon onion powder

1 teaspoon garlic powder

1 teaspoon dried basil

FOR THE PASTA

1 pound spaghetti

4. Check to see if the meatballs are cooked through by removing one meatball with a fork and putting it on a plate. Cut it in half. If no pink remains, the meatballs are done. If not, continue to cook them for a few more minutes. When the meatballs are done, turn off the heat and let everything cool a little.

5. Meanwhile, open the cans of tomato sauce, crushed or diced tomatoes, and tomato paste with the can opener and dump them into a large pot. Add the Italian seasoning, onion powder, garlic powder, and dried basil and stir together with a mixing spoon until combined. Put the pot on a burner on the stove, turn the heat to medium, and cook, stirring, until the sauce starts to bubble, about 5 minutes.

6. Carefully add the meatballs and onions to the sauce and stir until combined well. Reduce the heat to medium-low heat and continue to cook, stirring frequently, until everything is heated through.

7. Meanwhile, cook the spaghetti in the other large pot according to the package instructions. When the spaghetti is ready, wearing oven mitts, take the hot pot to the sink and drain the pasta in the colander (have an adult do this for you).

8. Serve the spaghetti topped with the meatballs and onions in the sauce.

Kid-Friendly Broccoli

By Will

Skill > Moderate

Most kids don't like broccoli. But when you do it right, with the perfect amount of butter and salt, instead of hating it, you will be loving it. This is the only broccoli I really enjoy.

ACTIVE TIME: 15 minutes > TOTAL TIME: 15 minutes > MAKES: 9 servings

Equipment

Cutting board

Chef's knife

Large pot with a lid

Fork

Colander

Oven mitts

Large serving bowl

Measuring spoons

Tongs

Ingredients

4½ heads broccoli

6 tablespoons extra virgin
olive oil or butter

¾ teaspoon coarse sea salt

1. Working on a cutting board and using a chef's knife, cut the broccoli into florets, discarding the heavy stalks, and put the florets into a large pot. Add ½ inch of water to the pot (you don't want to cover the broccoli with water, you just want it to sit in the water). Cover the pan with a lid.

2. Put the pot on a burner on the stove and turn the heat to high. Bring the water to a boil and cook the broccoli, covered, for 2–3 minutes, until it turns bright green and just becomes tender (pierce one floret with a fork to see if it is soft enough).

3. Put a colander in the sink. When the broccoli is just tender, put on the oven mitts and carefully transfer the pot to the sink (have an adult do this for you). Drain the broccoli in the colander.

4. Dump the drained broccoli into a large serving bowl. Drizzle with the olive oil, sprinkle with the sea salt, and toss with tongs to combine.

GRILLED CHEESE

By Paul

This is kind of a simple recipe, but I thought it would be cool to add a few optional toppings that you might not have thought of before, as well as some info on different kinds of cheese (see the box on the next page).

ACTIVE TIME: 15–18 minutes > TOTAL TIME: 15–18 minutes > MAKES: 1 sandwich for 1–2 servings

EQUIPMENT

Plate

Butter knife

Cutting board

Serrated knife

Paring knife

Skillet or griddle

Spatula

INGREDIENTS
(FOR 1 SANDWICH)

2 slices of bread

1 tablespoon butter, softened

1 small Roma tomato, thinly sliced

2–3 ounces cheese of choice (see the box on the next page for info on cheeses)

Optional toppings: salsa, sour cream, guacamole, dill pickle slices

1. Lay the two pieces of bread on a plate. With a butter knife, butter just the top of one of them with half of the butter.

2. On a cutting board with a serrated knife, thinly slice the tomato. Decide which kind of cheese you'd like to use (see the box on the next page), then, with a paring knife, thinly slice the cheese.

3. Put the slices of cheese on the non-buttered slice of bread neatly, covering all the bread space.

4. Lay 2–4 slices of tomato on top of the cheese. Place the buttered piece of bread on top of the tomatoes and cheese with the buttered side facing up.

5. Put a skillet or griddle on a burner on the stove and turn the heat to medium-low or low. Lay the sandwich in the skillet with the buttered side facing down.

6. While the sandwich is cooking, using the butter knife, carefully spread the remaining butter on the top slice of bread.

7. After about a minute, depending on how high the heat is and how thin or thick the bread is, check the bottom of the grilled cheese sandwich with a spatula. If it's brown, carefully flip it with the spatula. If not, let it cook a little longer, then flip. (If both sides of the sandwich are brown but the cheese isn't melted, put a lid on the pan for a few moments or turn the heat to all the way down to low and keep flipping it.)

8. When both sides are nicely browned and the cheese is melted, transfer the grilled cheese back to the plate and serve with optional toppings, if you'd like. Just open up the sandwich and add them.

THE BEST CHEESES TO USE FOR GRILLED CHEESE SANDWICHES

Out of all the common cheeses, mozzarella is the cheesiest; pepper Jack and Monterey Jack melt the quickest and have a stronger flavor; provolone also has a strong flavor, but melts slower; Havarti melts about as fast as provolone but doesn't have as strong a flavor. Sharp Cheddar cheese has a little bit more flavor than mild Cheddar cheese, but both are classic.

Pinto Gallo (Gallo Pinto)

By Paul

Skill > Advanced

This beans and rice dish from Central America is really called Gallo Pinto, but when we first started making it, I would always forget which word went first, so I called it Pinto Gallo. Traditionally, the dish is enjoyed for breakfast, so if you have leftovers from dinner, you could heat them up for breakfast!

ACTIVE TIME: 25–35 minutes > TOTAL TIME: 40–50 minutes > MAKES: about 6 servings

Equipment

Cutting board

Chef's knife

Measuring cups and spoons

Medium pot with a lid

Mixing spoon

Colander

Can opener

1. On a cutting board with a chef's knife, peel, crush, and mince the garlic cloves. Peel the onion. Dice the onion and bell pepper.

2. Put the onion, bell pepper, and olive oil in a medium pot. Put the pot on a burner on the stove and turn the heat to medium. Cook the onions and bell peppers, stirring constantly with the mixing spoon, until soft.

3. Add the garlic, rice, salt, and pepper (if using) and stir until the rice is toasted, then add the water or broth and stir to combine.

4. Put a colander in the sink. Open the cans of beans with the can opener. Add the beans to the colander, then rinse in cold running water until the water runs clear and drain. Dump the beans into the rice mixture in the pot, add the bay leaf, and increase the heat to high. When the mixture starts to boil, reduce the heat to low, put the lid on the pot, and simmer for 15 minutes.

5. After 15 minutes, check to see if the rice is done by pushing one grain against the side of the pot. If it breaks in half, it is done. Remove the bay leaf.

6. Serve with the toppings of your choice.

Ingredients

- 3 garlic cloves
- 1 large onion
- 1 sweet bell pepper
- ¼ cup olive oil
- 2 cups white rice
- 1 teaspoon salt
- ¼ teaspoon black pepper (optional)
- 4 cups water or chicken broth
- 2 (15-ounce) cans pinto beans
- 1 bay leaf
- Toppings of choice: salsa, cheese, cheese sauce, fried egg, avocado chunks, guacamole, sour cream, chips

CRISPY, CRUNCHY POTATOES

By Abigail

Skill > Advanced

Crispy, yummy, salty, flavorful—I can't live without these potatoes, and my entire family agrees . . . they're the best!

ACTIVE TIME: 10 minutes > TOTAL TIME: 30 minutes > MAKES: 5 servings

EQUIPMENT

Cutting board

Chef's knife

Large baking dish

Measuring cups and
  spoons

Oven mitts

Fork

INGREDIENTS

2 pounds potatoes

¼ cup olive oil

1 tablespoon dried
  oregano

1 tablespoon thyme

1 tablespoon basil

1 teaspoon salt

1. Preheat the oven to 400°F.

2. Working on a cutting board and using a chef's knife, cut the potatoes into 1-inch chunks and put them in a baking dish large enough to fit the chunks in a single layer (try not to have potatoes laying on each other if you can help it).

3. Add the olive oil, oregano, thyme, basil, and salt to the dish and toss everything together with your clean hands to coat the potatoes. Wash and dry your hands.

4. Wearing oven mitts, put the baking dish into the hot oven and bake the potatoes for 20 minutes, or until they are crispy and brown. If they don't look crispy on top, keep them in the oven for another 5 minutes and check on them again.

5. When they look done, put on your oven mitts and remove the dish from the oven, transferring it to a cool burner on the stove. With a fork, pierce one of the potato pieces. If it is soft and easy to get through without effort (using the fork), it's done. If not, reduce the oven temperature to 300°F and return the dish to the oven to cook 5 minutes more, or until done.

Oven-Roasted Green Beans

By Anthony   **Skill > Advanced**

Green beans are one of the first things I learned how to cook. One year, we had so many growing in our garden that we ate them all the time.

ACTIVE TIME: 5 minutes > TOTAL TIME: 30 minutes > MAKES: 5–6 servings

Equipment

Large rimmed baking
  sheet
Measuring spoons
Oven mitts

Ingredients

1 pound fresh green
  beans
2 tablespoons olive oil
½ teaspoon sea salt or
  Himalayan salt
½ teaspoon pepper
½ teaspoon onion powder
½ teaspoon garlic powder
  (optional)
2 tablespoons Parmesan
  cheese
Butter and dried lemon
  powder, for serving
  (optional)

1. Preheat the oven to 450°F.

2. Put the green beans on a large rimmed baking sheet. Drizzle the beans with the olive oil and sprinkle with the sea salt, pepper, onion powder, and garlic powder (if using). Toss the mixture with your clean hands until the beans are coated with the mixture. Spread the beans out evenly on the sheet. Wash your hands before you go on with the recipe.

3. Wearing oven mitts, place the baking sheet in the hot oven and roast the beans for 18–20 minutes, or until crispy and brown spots appear.

4. Wearing oven mitts, take the sheet out of the oven and put it on a cool burner on the stove. Sprinkle the Parmesan cheese over the beans and return the sheet to the oven. Roast the beans for 5 minutes more.

5. Wearing oven mitts, remove the beans from the oven. Serve with butter and a bit of dried lemon powder, if desired.

Oven-Baked Sweet Potato Fries

By Anthony

Skill > Advanced

One year, we grew over 300 pounds of sweet potatoes in our garden. We had a huge wire basket of them in our pantry all winter long and learned how to make sweet potatoes in so many ways. This one is my favorite!

ACTIVE TIME: 15 minutes > TOTAL TIME: 1 hour > MAKES: 1–2 servings

Equipment

Cutting board

Chef's knife

Large rimmed baking sheet

Measuring spoons

Oven mitts

Spatula

Ingredients

1 sweet potato

3 tablespoons olive oil

1 tablespoon coconut aminos or soy sauce

2 teaspoons onion powder

1 teaspoon garlic powder

2 teaspoons salt

½ teaspoon pepper

1. Preheat the oven to 375°F.

2. Working on a cutting board and using a chef's knife, cut the sweet potato lengthwise into about 20 thin slices. Transfer the potato slices to a large rimmed baking sheet and sprinkle them with the olive oil, coconut aminos or soy sauce, onion powder, garlic powder, salt, and pepper. Toss everything together with your clean hands until the potatoes are coated. Arrange the slices on the baking sheet in a single layer (try not to have the sweet potatoes laying on each other if you can help it). Wash your hands before you go on with the recipe.

3. Wearing oven mitts, put the baking sheet into the hot oven and bake the sweet potato fries, flipping them occasionally with a spatula, for 45 minutes, or until golden. Note: these fries will be soft because they are baked, not fried.

4. Wearing oven mitts, remove the baking sheet from the hot oven and serve the fries while they are warm. Garnish with fresh parsley, if you like.

Coconut Chicken Nuggets

By Will

Skill > Advanced

Yes, these are chicken nuggets—with a twist! The addition of coconut goes surprisingly well with the delicious taste of the chicken. This is one of my favorite recipes just because it's a common kid comfort food, with a slightly unusual taste.

ACTIVE TIME: 35 minutes > TOTAL TIME: 35 minutes > MAKES: 8 servings

EQUIPMENT

Oven-proof plate
  or platter
Medium mixing bowl
Whisk or fork
Large mixing bowl
Mixing spoon
Cutting board
Chef's knife
Large skillet
Tongs
Slotted spoon

1. Preheat the oven to 200°F and put an oven-proof plate or platter in the oven. (This will allow you to cook the chicken in batches and keep the chicken warm.)

2. Crack the eggs into a medium bowl, then using a whisk or a fork, whisk the eggs and set aside.

3. In a large mixing bowl, add the coconut flour, shredded coconut, garlic powder, onion powder, sea salt, and pepper, and stir with a mixing spoon to combine. Set aside.

4. Working on a cutting board and using a chef's knife, cut the chicken into bite-size pieces.

5. Transfer the chicken to the bowl of beaten eggs and toss with your hands to coat. Add the egg-coated chicken to the flour mixture and toss with your hands until the pieces are completely coated. Since you have been handling chicken, wash your hands before continuing with the recipe.

6. Put a large skillet on a burner on the stove and turn the heat to medium-high. Add about half of the coconut oil. When it is hot and shimmering (but not smoking), cook the chicken in small batches, using tongs to turn the pieces, until browned on all sides and

INGREDIENTS

3 eggs

1¼ cups coconut flour

½ cup shredded coconut

2¼ teaspoons garlic powder

2¼ teaspoons onion powder

2¼ teaspoons sea salt

¾ teaspoon ground black pepper

2¼ pounds boneless chicken breasts

9 tablespoons coconut oil

Ranch dressing, for dipping

cooked through. As the chicken is cooked, transfer it with a slotted spoon to the warm plate in the oven. Add a few more tablespoons of additional oil to the skillet and continue to cook the remaining chicken in the same way.

7. Serve the chicken nuggets with ranch dressing for dipping.

LIME-MARINATED STEAK

By Will

Skill > Advanced

I love steak and am always asking my mom and dad if I can make this delicious recipe.

ACTIVE TIME: 15 minutes > TOTAL TIME: 85 minutes > MAKES: 4 servings

EQUIPMENT

Cutting board

Chef's knife

Citrus juicer

Vegetable peeler

Grater

Measuring spoons

Shallow dish

Plastic wrap

Charcoal or gas grill,
   or large cast-iron skillet

Meat thermometer

Cutting board or
   serving platter

1. Working on a cutting board and using a chef's knife, cut the limes into halves. Using a citrus juicer, juice the limes.

2. Working on a cutting board and using a chef's knife, mince the scallions.

3. With a vegetable peeler, peel the ginger, then, with a grater, finely grate the ginger.

4. Add the lime juice, scallions, ginger, soy sauce, and red pepper flakes to a shallow dish and stir to combine. Place the flank steak in the mixture, turning it over to coat, cover with plastic wrap, and refrigerate for at least 1 hour or overnight.

5. Thirty minutes before grilling, take the meat out of the refrigerator and let it come to room temperature.

6. *To cook the steak on a charcoal or gas grill:* Heat the grill to high heat. You should be able to hold your hand about an inch over the grill grate for only 1 second before it feels too hot.

7. Place the steak on the hot grill (discard the marinade) and sear it on each side about 3–7 minutes, depending how cooked you want your steak to be. Use a meat thermometer to measure the center temperature: rare = 125°F, medium rare = 135°F, medium = 145°F.

   NOTE: *Do not take a flank steak past medium as it will continue to cook when taken off the heat source. Now, skip to step 11.*

INGREDIENTS

4 limes

2 scallions

1-inch piece of fresh ginger

2 tablespoons soy sauce

¼ teaspoon red pepper flakes

1½ pounds flank steak

Coarse sea salt

Ground black pepper

1–2 tablespoons tallow and/or coconut oil, if you're cooking the steak in a cast-iron skillet

1–2 tablespoons butter, if you're cooking the steak in a cast-iron skillet

8. *To cook the steak in a large cast-iron skillet:* Remove the flank steak from the marinade, allow it to come to room temperature, then pat dry any surface moisture with paper towels.

9. Coat both sides of the steak liberally with coarse sea salt and ground black pepper. Be generous. You are creating a crust.

10. Put a cast-iron skillet on a burner on the stove and turn the heat to high until the skillet is searing hot. Add the tallow or coconut oil and butter (the tallow or coconut oil will keep the butter from burning, but if you are dairy-free just use all coconut oil or tallow). Just before the oil begins to smoke, lay the steak in the pan and allow it to sear on each side undisturbed for 3–7 minutes, depending on the level of doneness you desire. Use a meat thermometer to measure the center temperature: rare = 125°F, medium rare = 135°F, medium = 145°F.

NOTE: *Do not take a flank steak past medium, as it will continue to cook when taken off the heat source.*

11. Place the cooked flank steak on a cutting board or serving platter and leave it undisturbed for 10 minutes. This will allow the juices to run back into the meat instead of escaping.

12. Slice the steak in thin strips across the grain and serve.

FISH TACOS

By Will

Skill > Advanced

Fish tacos are my favorite seafood dish. The warm taco shell and delicious taste of fresh caught, perfectly cooked fish gets me every time.

ACTIVE TIME: 45 minutes > TOTAL TIME: 45 minutes > MAKES: 4 servings

EQUIPMENT

Measuring cups and spoons
Small bowl
Mixing spoon
Baking dish
Brush for oiling the fish
Cutting board
Chef's knife
Citrus juicer
Oven mitts
Large serving bowl
Tongs
Aluminum foil
Oven-proof platter
Large skillet
Forks

1. Preheat the oven to 375°F.

2. Make the spice mix: Put the oregano, chili powder, garlic powder, coriander, cumin, and sea salt in a small bowl and stir to combine.

3. Prepare and bake the fish: Place the fish in a baking dish, brush with the olive oil, then sprinkle evenly with the spice mix. Using a cutting board and chef's knife, cut 2 of the limes in half. Using a citrus juicer, juice 2 of the limes and sprinkle half of the juice over the fish. Wearing oven mitts, put the baking dish in the hot oven and bake the fish, uncovered, about 10 minutes.

4. While the fish bakes, make the slaw. On a cutting board with a chef's knife, thinly shred the red cabbage and transfer to a large bowl. Cut the green onions into small pieces and add to the bowl. Halve the jalapeño and remove the seeds, then mince half of the jalapeño and transfer to the bowl (reserve the other half for another recipe). (Remember: Don't touch your eyes after touching the jalapeños.) Add the remaining half of the lime juice from the fish preparation, then add sea salt and pepper to taste. Toss the slaw with tongs and set aside.

5. When the fish is done, turn the oven off. Wearing oven mitts, remove the baking dish from the oven and place it on a cool burner on the stove. Put a piece of aluminum foil over the fish to keep it warm. Put an ovenproof platter in the still warm oven. You will use this platter to hold the warmed tortillas.

Ingredients

FOR THE SPICE MIX

½ teaspoon dried oregano

½ teaspoon chili powder

½ teaspoon garlic powder

½ teaspoon coriander

¼ teaspoon ground cumin

1 teaspoon coarse sea salt

FOR THE FISH

1 pound halibut or any firm white fish

1 tablespoon olive oil

2 limes to juice and 2 limes for serving

FOR THE SLAW

¼ small red cabbage

4 green onions

1 jalapeño pepper

Coarse sea salt, to taste

Ground black pepper, to taste

FOR ASSEMBLY

8 coconut flour tortillas

2 tablespoons coconut oil, plus more as needed

½ cup cilantro

6. Warm the tortillas: Put a large skillet on a burner on the stove and turn the heat to medium-low. Add 2 tablespoons of the coconut oil to the pan and swirl the pan to coat. Place the tortillas, one at a time, in the pan to warm them, transferring them as warmed to the platter in the warm oven. Add more oil to the pan as needed.

7. Assemble and serve the tacos: On a cutting board with the chef's knife, chop the cilantro and cut the remaining 2 limes into wedges. With two forks, gently separate the fish in the baking dish into large chunks. Wearing oven mitts, take the warm tortillas out of the oven. Put the dinner plates on the counter. Put a tortilla on each plate and top each one with some of the fish, slaw, and cilantro. Serve the tacos with a wedge of lime on the side.

Mediterranean Sun-Dried Tomato Chicken

By Katie

I love how pretty this dish is, but it's even tastier than it looks! A coating of tangy sun-dried tomatoes, creamy mozzarella, pine nuts, and fresh parsley makes the chicken super tender and flavorful.

ACTIVE TIME: 10 minutes > TOTAL TIME: 35–40 minutes > MAKES: 4 servings

Equipment

Medium baking dish
Food processor
Measuring cups and spoons
Rubber scraper
Oven mitts
Paring knife

Ingredients

1 pound boneless, skinless chicken breasts

½ cup sun-dried tomatoes, packed in olive oil

½ cup fresh parsley

¼ cup pine nuts

¼ cup grated mozzarella or dairy-free mozzarella

¼ cup olive oil or avocado oil

½ teaspoon garlic powder

⅛ teaspoon salt

1. Preheat the oven to 350°F.

2. Place the chicken in a medium baking dish and set aside.

3. Put the food processor on the counter and add the tomatoes, parsley, pine nuts, mozzarella, oil, garlic powder, and salt to the food processor. Pulse the ingredients a few times until the mixture looks like a paste with little pieces of nuts and parsley mixed in.

4. Unplug the processor. Scoop the tomato mixture out of the food processor with a rubber scraper and place it on top of the chicken. Use clean hands to pat the mixture so that it coats the top of the chicken evenly. Wash your hands.

5. Wearing oven mitts, put the baking dish into the hot oven and bake the chicken for 25–30 minutes, or until fully cooked.

6. Wearing oven mitts, remove the baking dish from the oven and place on a potholder. Check to see if the chicken is fully cooked by cutting through the thickest part of the breast with a paring knife. If it is white all the way through, it's done. If any pink remains, return the baking dish to the oven for 5 minutes more and check again.

HONEY-MUSTARD CHICKEN

By Katie

Skill > Advanced

Here's a great way to change up plain ol' chicken! This tangy, sweet recipe is a definite favorite in my house. My little brothers love that it's tender and juicy, and I love that it's made in one pan so there's less to clean up after dinner.

ACTIVE TIME: 5 minutes > TOTAL TIME: 30–35 minutes > MAKES: 4 servings

EQUIPMENT

Medium baking dish
   (2½-quart)

Small bowl

Measuring cups and
   spoons

Fork

Spoon

Oven mitts

Paring knife

Large potholder

INGREDIENTS

1½ pounds boneless,
   skinless chicken breasts

¼ cup whole grain mustard

¼ cup honey

1 tablespoon avocado
   or olive oil

¼ teaspoon garlic powder

1 teaspoon dried
   rosemary

⅛ teaspoon salt

Ground black pepper,
   to taste

1. Preheat the oven to 375°F.

2. Place the chicken breasts in a medium baking dish.

3. In a small bowl, add the mustard, honey, oil, garlic powder, rosemary, and salt and stir together with a fork. Pour the honey-mustard mixture over the top of the chicken breasts, then use a spoon to spread it around. Make sure all the chicken is covered.

4. Wearing oven mitts, place the baking dish in the hot oven and bake the chicken for 25–30 minutes, or until it is cooked through. To check, wearing oven mitts, remove the dish from the oven and put it on the potholder. With a paring knife, cut through the thickest part of the breast. If it is white all the way through, it's done. If any pink remains, return the baking dish to the oven for 5 minutes more and check again.

5. Sprinkle the chicken with a little black pepper and serve, drizzled with some of the pan liquid.

Cheesy Beef, Potato, & Carrot Casserole

By Paul

You'll probably want to make this recipe on the weekend when you have lots of time, but it's really delicious and worth the effort. If it's difficult for you to cut a lot of big, round veggies (the carrots and the potatoes) the first few times, and you don't have a food processor, get the whole family to pitch in.

ACTIVE TIME: 15–20 minutes > TOTAL TIME: 75–110 minutes > MAKES: 4–6 servings

Equipment

Cutting board

Chef's knife

Large pot

Spatula

Food processor (optional)

Jar with a tight-fitting lid

Measuring cups and spoons

9- by 13-inch baking dish

Ladle

Oven mitts

Fork

(Ingredients list is on the following page)

1. Working on a cutting board and using a chef's knife, peel, crush, and mince the garlic cloves and set aside.

2. Put a large pot on a burner on the stove and turn the heat to medium. Add the ground beef and cook, chopping up the meat into small pieces with a spatula until brown and no pink remains. Drain off the grease, leaving a little bit in the pot (ask an adult to do this for you).

3. On the cutting board with the chef's knife, peel and cut the onion into small pieces. Add the onion and the minced garlic to the beef and continue to cook, stirring occasionally, until the onion is translucent.

4. Put a food processor on the counter and attach the slicing attachment. With the processor turned on, feed the carrots through the funnel tube with the plunger to thinly slice them. (Or, just cut up the carrots on the cutting board with the chef's knife into very thin rounds.) Add the carrot slices to the beef mixture.

5. Add 4 tablespoons of butter to the beef mixture and stir until the butter is melted. Then add 2½ cups of the milk and continue to cook, stirring occasionally.

(continued)

INGREDIENTS

3 cloves garlic

1 pound ground beef

1 medium onion

4 medium carrots

4 tablespoons butter, plus more to butter the baking dish

3 cups milk

2 tablespoons arrowroot powder (or 4½ teaspoons cornstarch)

2½ cups shredded cheese (Cheddar, mozzarella, Monterey jack)

1 teaspoon salt

½ teaspoon black pepper

2 teaspoons Italian seasoning

½ cup frozen peas (optional)

About 4 large potatoes or 6 small ones, peeled or unpeeled, cut lengthwise into strips

6. Meanwhile, in a jar with a tight-fitting lid, add the remaining ½ cup of the milk and the arrowroot powder. Put the lid on and shake until mixed well.

7. When the beef mixture just comes to a boil, pour in the arrowroot mixture, reduce the heat to low, and stir until it thickens.

8. Add 1½ cups of the cheese and stir until it is melted. Add the salt, pepper, Italian seasoning, and peas (if using). Remove the pot from the heat.

9. Using the food processor with the slicing attachment, turn the processor on and feed the potato strips through the funnel tube with the plunger to thinly slice them. (Or just use a cutting board and chef's knife and cut them into very thin rounds.) Turn the processor off and carefully transfer the potato slices (you should have about 10 cups) to the cutting board.

10. Arrange an oven rack in the middle of the oven, then preheat the oven to 400°F. Grease a 9- by 13-inch baking dish with butter.

11. Layer the potatoes and cheesy-beef mixture in the baking dish (you will have 4 layers total). Arrange half of the sliced potatoes (about 5 cups) into the bottom of the dish, then use a large ladle to spread half of the cheesy-beef mixture evenly on top of the potatoes. Now arrange another layer of the remaining potatoes on top of the beef. Finally top the casserole with the remaining beef mixture.

12. Wearing oven mitts, put the baking dish on the middle rack in the hot oven and bake the casserole for 40 minutes if you used a food processor for the carrots and potatoes or 65 minutes if you cut them by hand.

13. Wearing oven mitts, take the baking dish out of the oven and put it on top of a cold burner on the stovetop. Sprinkle the remaining 1 cup of the cheese over the top of the casserole. Return the dish to the oven for 5 minutes more.

14. Wearing oven mitts, take the baking dish out of the oven again and check to see if the casserole is done: poke a fork into the casserole. If the potatoes are soft, it is done. If not, return the baking dish to the oven for 5–20 minutes more.

15. Serve the casserole while it is nice and hot. Individual servings may need more salt and pepper.

SUBSTITUTIONS

Ground sausage may be used instead of the ground beef. Also, you can use lots of other vegetables, like parsnips, zucchini, or even a cucumber instead of carrots. And feel free to put more cheese on top of the dish if you think that there isn't enough.

Snacks

Gluten-Free Puffy Snack Mix >>> 138

Trail Mix >>> 139

Bacon-Wrapped Dates >>> 140

Strawberry–Chia Seed Jam >>> 143

Blueberry-Banana Ice Pops >>> 144

Pineapple-Lemon Ice Pops >>> 145

Berry Yogurt Ice Pops >>> 146

Monkey Salad >>> 147

Guacamole >>> 149

Plantain Chips >>> 150

White Hot Chocolate >>> 151

Taco Cheese Sauce >>> 153

Maple Granola >>> 155

Garlic Beef Jerky >>> 156

Banana Bread >>> 159

Buffalo Wings >>> 160

"Cornbread" Muffins >>> 163

Blender Bread >>> 164

Cinnamon Raisin Bread with Cream Cheese Glaze >>> 166

Kale Chips >>> 168

Easy, Cheesy Popcorn >>> 169

Gluten-Free Puffy Snack Mix

By Abigail

Skill > Easy

This creamy, nutty, sweet mixture has a spot in my heart. I hope it has one in yours, too.

ACTIVE TIME: 10 minutes > **TOTAL TIME:** 10 minutes > **MAKES:** 6 servings

Equipment

Large mixing bowl

Measuring spoons

Mixing spoon

Plastic wrap (optional)

Ingredients

¼ cup almond butter

2 teaspoons honey

2 teaspoons shredded coconut, plus extra to coat the balls

1 teaspoon almond flour

1 tablespoon softened butter

2 cups puffed rice cereal

1. In a large bowl, add the almond butter, honey, 2 teaspoons of coconut, almond flour, and butter and stir together with a mixing spoon until smooth and creamy. Spread the mixture onto the bottom of the bowl.

2. Add 1 cup of the cereal to the bowl and then stir it in until combined well. Add the remaining cup of cereal and stir it again.

3. Eat this right away with some milk or a creamy drink, or put it in the refrigerator, covered with plastic wrap, until you are ready to eat it.

Tip

For an option that includes gluten, add some crushed-up pretzels to give your snack a nice sweet and salty flavor. How many you add is totally up to you.

TRAIL MIX

By Paul   Skill > Easy

Everyone loves trail mix, and it doesn't have to come in a plastic bag. Now you can make your own. Just remember not to eat too much of this! Nuts will fill you up quickly.

ACTIVE TIME: 1 minute > TOTAL TIME: 2 minutes > MAKES: 1 serving

EQUIPMENT

1 small bowl

INGREDIENTS

Almonds

Cashews

Raisins

Macadamia nuts

Walnuts

Pecans

Dried figs

Prunes

Dried Apricots

Coconut flakes

— There aren't any measurements listed with the ingredients because you should make this recipe any way you want to. All of these ingredients are optional, but I recommend at least two kinds of nuts, especially if you are going to use any dried fruit. Personally, I add a small handful (slightly more than 2 tablespoons) of almonds, cashews, raisins, and a sprinkle of coconut flakes to a small bowl. That's it!

Tip

This trail mix can be doubled, tripled, or otherwise multiplied to your heart's desire and enjoyed over several days. Just remember that all nuts should be stored in a cool place, and they don't keep forever. Look at the "use by" date on the bags of the ingredients and eat it up before then.

BACON-WRAPPED DATES

By Abigail

This recipe was inspired by a restaurant that served them to my family. We thought they were so good, we devoured about three orders by the time we left!

ACTIVE TIME: 10 minutes > **TOTAL TIME: 30 minutes** > **MAKES: 16 stuffed dates (about 8 servings)**

EQUIPMENT

Small bowl

16 toothpicks

Cutting board

Paring knife

Rimmed baking sheet

Oven mitts

Cooling rack

INGREDIENTS

8 slices bacon
(make sure it isn't
smoked or flavored)

16 Medjool dates
(buy these since they
are bigger)

4 ounces goat cheese

1. Fill a small bowl with water and soak 16 toothpicks in the water. We will be putting the toothpicks in the oven and, since wood is flammable (which means it can catch on fire), want to soak them to be extra safe.

2. Preheat the oven to 350°F.

3. Working on a cutting board and using a paring knife, cut the 8 bacon pieces crosswise in half (leaving you with 16 half pieces) and set the pieces aside.

4. Using a paring knife, put one date on the board with one of the ends facing you. Cut a small slit into the date the long way to remove the pit, but don't cut it all the way through (or you won't be able to stuff it with the yummy cheese). Make a small slit in the remaining dates in the same way.

5. Working with one date at a time, take a small piece of goat cheese and stuff it into the middle of the date. Squish the date a little to make it look like a normal date again. Stuff the remaining dates in the same way.

6. Working with one stuffed date and one piece of bacon at a time, place the date toward the end of one piece of bacon and roll it up. Stick a wet toothpick into the end of the bacon and through the date to secure the bacon to the date. Wrap and secure all the dates in the same way.

7. Transfer all the stuffed dates (toothpicks included) to a rimmed baking sheet.

8. Wearing oven mitts, put the baking sheet in the hot oven and bake the dates for 10 minutes.

9. Wearing oven mitts, transfer the baking sheet to a cool burner on top of the stove and flip over the dates so that the bacon can cook evenly. Put the baking sheet back in the oven and bake the dates for another 10 minutes.

10. Using oven mitts, take the baking sheet out of the oven and put it on a cooling rack. Let the dates cool for 5 minutes, then serve.

STRAWBERRY—CHIA SEED JAM

By Katie

Skill > Easy

Most jams are loaded with tons of processed sugar, but this strawberry jam is naturally sweetened with maple syrup. It's super yummy in my Peanut Butter & Jelly Cups (page 173), but you can also spread it on homemade Blender Bread (page 164), "Cornbread" Muffins (page 163), or whatever sounds yummy to you!

ACTIVE TIME: 20 minutes > TOTAL TIME: 2 hours 25 minute > MAKES: about 1 pint

EQUIPMENT

Medium bowl
Medium pot
Potato masher
Measuring spoons
Mixing spoon
Pint jar with a lid

INGREDIENTS

1 pound strawberries, fresh or frozen (about 3 cups)

5 tablespoons maple syrup

5 tablespoons chia seeds

3–4 drops natural red food coloring (optional)

1. If you're using fresh strawberries, remove the leaves and stems. If you're using frozen strawberries, put them in a bowl on the counter and allow them to thaw a little. When they're soft enough to mash, proceed to the next step.

2. Place the strawberries in a medium pot, and mash them with a potato masher until they're the consistency of coarse applesauce. Add the maple syrup.

3. Put the pot on a burner on the stove and turn the heat to medium-high. Bring the strawberry mixture just to a boil, then immediately reduce the heat to low/medium heat and simmer for 10 minutes, stirring with the mixing spoon every 2–3 minutes.

4. Remove the pot from the heat and stir in the chia seeds and food coloring (if using). Allow the jam to cool in the pot for 5 minutes.

5. Pour the cooled jam into a pint jar and put in the refrigerator to thicken for at least 2 hours before using. Once it is chilled, put the lid on the jar. Serve as a spread on slices of Blender Bread or your favorite crackers.

BLUEBERRY-BANANA ICE POPS

By Paul

Skill > Easy

When I was younger, I loved going on scavenger hunts and searching for treasure in my backyard. And I always loved finding the "hidden treasures" at the bottom of a fruit ice pop. Now you want to know what the hidden treasures are here, right? Go on, make the recipe and you'll find out!

ACTIVE TIME: 5–10 minutes > **TOTAL TIME: 5–10 minutes + overnight freezing** > **MAKES: 4 servings**

EQUIPMENT

Blender

Measuring cups and spoons

4 ice pop molds or an ice cube tray

INGREDIENTS

1 cup milk

1 banana (can be frozen)

1½ cups frozen blueberries

2 tablespoons honey

1. Put a blender on your counter. Put the milk, banana, 1 cup of the blueberries, and honey into the blender, and put the lid on tightly.

2. Blend the mixture on high speed if you have a low-power blender and medium if you have a high-power blender until there are no chunks, about 30–60 seconds.

3. Put 3–4 of the remaining blueberries into each of 4 ice pop molds or a few in each ice cube tray compartment.

4. Pour the blender mixture into your molds or the ice cube tray, and put in the freezer until frozen, overnight or for 12–14 hours.

Pineapple-Lemon Ice Pops

By Paul

Skill > Easy

I was experimenting with ice pop recipes, and I realized that adding lemon to the pineapple ice pop mixture made it way better. This is my personal favorite ice pop recipe of all time!

ACTIVE TIME: 5 minutes > **TOTAL TIME: 5 minutes + overnight freezing** > **MAKES: about 4 servings**

Equipment

Blender

Measuring cups and spoons

4 ice pop molds or an ice cube tray

Ingredients

1 cup plain yogurt

1 cup frozen pineapple pieces

2 tablespoons cup raw honey

2 tablespoons lemon juice

Tip

If you are not a yogurt fan, or don't want the ice pops to taste too strongly of yogurt, you can use a little less yogurt in the fruit mixture.

---

1. Put the blender on the counter. Add the yogurt, pineapple, and honey into the blender. Just before you blend the mixture, add the lemon juice (this will prevent the acid in it from curdling the yogurt).

2. Blend the mixture on a high setting if you have a low-power blender and medium if you have a high-power blender until there are no chunks, 30–60 seconds, depending on how frozen your pineapple is and the thickness of your honey.

3. Pour the mixture into 4 ice pop molds or an ice cube tray, and put it in the freezer until frozen, overnight or for 12–14 hours.

Berry Yogurt Ice Pops

By Paul

Skill > Easy

I love making these ice pops in the summer because they're super refreshing and healthy, unlike super-sugary, yucky food coloring. Why not invite your friends over to make some?

ACTIVE TIME: 5–10 minutes > **TOTAL TIME: 5–10 minutes + overnight freezing** > **MAKES: 4 servings**

Equipment

Blender

Measuring cups and spoons

4 ice pop molds or an ice cube tray

Ingredients

1 cup plain yogurt

1 cup any mixed berries (frozen or fresh)

2 tablespoons raw honey

1. Put the blender on the counter. Put the yogurt, berries, and honey into the blender and put the lid on tightly.

2. Blend the mixture on the high setting if you have a low-power blender and on medium if you have a high-power blender until there are no chunks, about 20–25 seconds.

3. Pour the mixture into 4 ice pop molds or ice cube tray compartments and put in the freezer until frozen, overnight or for 12–14 hours.

MONKEY SALAD

 Paul

Skill > Easy

This is a super easy and simple snack recipe. Feel free to choose any of the ingredients listed. I usually just throw in a banana, a handful of whatever nuts are available, and some raisins and pour in some milk. You really don't have to measure.

ACTIVE TIME: 2–5 minutes > **TOTAL TIME: 2–5 minutes** > **MAKES: 1 serving**

EQUIPMENT

Cutting board

Butter knife

Small bowl

Measuring cups and
  spoons

INGREDIENTS

1 banana

¼ cup or less shredded
  coconut (optional)

¼ cup or less cashews
  (salted or not) (optional)

2 tablespoons or less
  almonds (optional)

2 tablespoons or less
  raisins (optional)

½ cup or less milk
  (optional)

1. Peel the banana. Working on a cutting board and using a butter knife, cut the banana into circles and put them in a small bowl.

2. Add the coconut, nuts (those listed or any others), and raisins and pour in the milk.

Tip

The guacamole will keep in the fridge for maybe a day or two, if you keep the surface covered with plastic wrap, but it gets brown pretty quickly, so try to eat it all on the day you make it.

GUACAMOLE

 By Paul   **Skill** > Easy

Way back, when I was eight or nine years old, I was really good at this recipe, but it was the only one I knew how to make—testimony to how easy this recipe is. I can tell you, though, it is totally worth making.

ACTIVE TIME: 5–10 minutes > TOTAL TIME: 5–10 minutes > MAKES: about 6 servings

EQUIPMENT

Cutting board
Chef's knife
Citrus juicer (optional)
Small bowl
Fork
Measuring spoons

INGREDIENTS

½ of a lime or
    1 tablespoon lime juice

1 avocado

¾–1 teaspoon adobo
    seasoning (or combine
    ¼ teaspoon oregano,
    ¼ teaspoon garlic
    powder, ¼ teaspoon
    onion powder,
    ⅛ teaspoon cumin,
    and ⅛ teaspoon black
    pepper)

¼ teaspoon salt

Diced tomato (optional)

1. Working on a cutting board and using a chef's knife, cut the lime in half. Using a citrus juicer, juice the lime into a small bowl.

2. Carefully use the tip of a chef's knife to make a slit in the avocado until the tip touches the pit. Then put the blade of the knife into the slit and turn the avocado around, creating a cut all the way around the avocado.

3. Put the knife down, twist the halves of the avocado in different directions, then pull apart the halves of the avocado.

4. Take the half that has the pit in it and carefully thwack the blade of the knife into the pit. Twist the knife so that the pit comes out. Carefully whack the handle of the knife against the side of your trash can until the pit falls into the trash.

5. Using a fork, make slits on the inside of the avocado halves, all the way to the skin. Scoop the mashed avocado into the small bowl with a fork.

6. Add the adobo seasoning and the salt to the avocado, and mix and mash it all together with the fork.

7. Top the guacamole with the diced tomato (if using), and serve with pretty much any raw vegetable, on tacos, or with other Mexican foods.

Plantain Chips

By Will

Skill > Moderate

Plantain chips, one of my favorite snacks, are so much better when they are homemade.

ACTIVE TIME: 10 minutes > TOTAL TIME: 10 minutes > MAKES: 6 servings

Equipment

Cutting board
Butter knife
Large frying pan
Measuring spoons
Spatula
Slotted spoon
Plate
Paper towels

Ingredients

3 green plantains
¼ cup coconut oil
Sea salt, to taste

1. Peel the plantains. Working on a cutting board and using a butter knife, cut them into thin rounds.

2. Put a large frying pan on a burner on the stove and turn the heat to medium-high. Add the coconut oil. When it is hot but not smoking, carefully add the plantain slices in a single layer. (If your pan is not big enough, you may need to fry the plantains in two batches.)

3. Fry the plantains until the edges are golden brown, about 1–2 minutes, then flip each slice with a spatula and cook for another 1–2 minutes on the other side. When the plantains are done, transfer them with a slotted spoon to a plate covered with paper towels to drain off any excess oil.

4. Sprinkle the slices with sea salt while the chips are still hot and serve.

WHITE HOT CHOCOLATE

By Katie

The creamy, milky goodness of this hot chocolate will warm you right up!

ACTIVE TIME: 10 minutes > **TOTAL TIME:** 10 minutes > **SERVES:** 1

EQUIPMENT

Small pot or saucepan
Measuring cup and spoon
Fork
Mug

INGREDIENTS

1 cup milk of choice
¼ cup white chocolate chips
¼ teaspoon vanilla

1. Put the milk, white chocolate chips, and vanilla in a small pot or saucepan.

2. Place the pot on the stove over medium heat. As the milk heats up, it will melt the chocolate chips. To evenly distribute the chocolate in the hot milk, stir the mixture with a fork until the chocolate chips have completely melted and the consistency of the mixture is smooth and thick.

3. Take the pot off the stove, and pour the steaming hot chocolate into your favorite mug.

Tip

The cheese sauce can be used over things other than tacos, like steamed broccoli, cauliflower, or even just boiled pasta. You can add 1 cup of mild, medium, or spicy salsa and 1 pound of cooked ground beef to the final cheese sauce, too, to use over tacos. Simply cook up the ground beef in a skillet before you start making the sauce and set it aside, or use leftover cooked ground beef from another recipe. Add the cooked beef to the cooked sauce as a final step, along with the salsa, if desired, and continue to cook everything over low heat until it is warmed through.

Taco Cheese Sauce

By Paul

Skill > Advanced

What kid doesn't like to put cheese sauce on just about everything? Of course, it is a must on tacos, but have a look at the picture for other ideas. Also, you should know that your cheese sauce is going to be less thick if you reheat it, so for maximum stringiness, make it right before you use it.

ACTIVE TIME: 30-35 minutes > TOTAL TIME: 30–35 minutes > MAKES: 6 servings

EQUIPMENT

Medium pot or large saucepan

Butter knife

Measuring cups and spoons

Wooden spoon

INGREDIENTS

3 cups milk

6 tablespoons butter

3 tablespoons arrowroot powder

3 cups shredded cheese (any kind, but Cheddar is good and mozzarella makes the cheese sauce super cheesy)

½ teaspoon ground cumin (optional)

1. Put a medium pot or large saucepan on a burner on the stove and turn the heat to medium-low. With a butter knife, add the butter to the pan and let it melt, stirring constantly with a wooden spoon. Add about 2½ cups of the milk, stirring to combine. Increase the heat to high, stirring constantly to avoid burning the milk. When the milk comes to a boil, reduce the heat to low heat.

2. Pour the remaining ½ cup of milk into a jar with a tightly fitting lid and add the arrowroot powder. Shake the jar until you can't see any lumps. (You are going to use this mixture to thicken the milk mixture before you add the cheese.)

3. Pour the milk and arrowroot mixture into the milk in the pan and increase the heat to high. Bring the mixture back to a boil, stirring occasionally, then reduce the heat to low and stir constantly until the mixture starts to thicken.

4. Add the cheese and stir until it melts into the thickened milk mixture. Add the cumin (if using) and stir until combined.

TO MAKE THE GRANOLA IN A DEHYDRATOR

Spread the granola mixture on the dehydrator tray and dehydrate for 8–10 hours at 110 degrees, or until it is dry and crunchy. Remove the granola from dehydrator, transfer it to a sealable container, and store it in the refrigerator.

MAPLE GRANOLA

By Katie

Skill > Advanced

Sweet and crunchy, this maple granola makes a yummy snack or breakfast. I like to pour a glass of almond milk over it and eat it like cereal. It can be made in the oven or a dehydrator, if you have one (see the box on the previous page for instructions).

ACTIVE TIME: 10 minutes > **TOTAL TIME: 30–35 minutes** > **MAKES: 3 servings**

EQUIPMENT

Parchment paper
Rimmed baking sheet
Food processor
Medium bowl
Wooden spoon
Oven mitts
Cooling rack
Airtight storage container
Dehydrator (optional)

INGREDIENTS

1 cup almonds
1 cup walnuts
½ cup sunflower seeds
1 cup large coconut flakes
¼ cup maple syrup
2 teaspoons vanilla extract
¼ teaspoon salt

1. Preheat the oven to 300°F. Place a piece of parchment paper on top of a rimmed baking sheet.

2. Put a food processor on the counter. Add the almonds, walnuts and sunflower seeds to the food processor and pulse a few times until chopped into medium pieces. Transfer the nut mixture to a medium bowl.

3. Add the coconut, maple syrup, vanilla, and salt to the nut mixture and, using the wooden spoon, stir until combined well.

4. Spread out the granola mixture evenly in the parchment-lined baking sheet.

5. Wearing oven mitts, put the baking sheet in the oven and bake the granola for 20–25 minutes, or until the coconut is very light golden brown on the edges.

6. Wearing oven mitts, remove the baking sheet from the oven and let it cool on a cooling rack for 15 minutes.

7. Using the wooden spoon, break the granola into pieces and store in an airtight container.

GARLIC BEEF JERKY

By Anthony

By Anthony

Skill > Advanced

Beef jerky is so delicious! I love to take it on camping trips, but it can be expensive and sometimes store-bought jerky has bad-for-you ingredients in it. This recipe is easy to make yourself, but slicing the meat thin enough can be tricky. Ask a butcher or other adult to help out with that. And, always remember to wash your hands really well after touching raw meat!

ACTIVE TIME: 15 minutes > **TOTAL TIME: 15 minutes + 4–8 hours baking time** > **MAKES: about 10 servings**

EQUIPMENT

Large bowl or container with a lid

Measuring cups and spoons

Whisk or mixing spoon

Plastic wrap

12 bamboo or metal skewers

Large rimmed baking sheet

Wire oven rack

Oven mitts

1. In a large bowl or a large storage container with a lid, add the coconut aminos, soy sauce, Worcestershire sauce, maple syrup, pepper, onion powder, garlic powder, and chili powder, and mix until combined well. Add the steak slices and mix until coated with the spicy mixture. Cover the bowl with plastic wrap or put the lid on the storage container (if using), and transfer to the refrigerator to let the meat marinate overnight.

2. If using bamboo skewers, soak them in cool water for at least 1 hour.

3. Put one oven rack on the lowest position in the oven and put a large rimmed baking sheet on it. Put the other rack on the highest position. Preheat the oven to its lowest temperature, usually 170°F.

4. Thread 8–10 pieces of the meat on a skewer by poking a hole through the meat at one end, allowing the pieces to hang down off of it. Fill up more skewers with all the remaining meat slices in the same way.

5. Have an adult help you out with this step. Wearing oven mitts, arrange these skewers on the higher oven rack so that the meat slices are hanging down in the middle of the oven over the baking sheet. (Or, you can lay the meat pieces flat on a wire rack that is then

INGREDIENTS

½ cup coconut aminos

½ cup soy sauce

½ cup Worcestershire sauce

¼ cup maple syrup

1 teaspoon ground black pepper

1 teaspoon onion powder

1 teaspoon garlic powder

1 teaspoon chili powder

3 pounds flank steak, cut into ¼-inch-thick slices (ask a butcher or other adult to cut the meat)

set on top of the baking sheet that is on the lower rack (the meat can't be flat on the baking sheet or they won't dry enough).

6. Bake the meat strips for 4–8 hours (depending on the thickness of the meat), until browned all the way through and dry, but still a little bit pliable.

7. Wearing oven mitts, carefully remove the strips from the oven and let them cool on a wire rack. You can store the jerky in storage containers in the refrigerator for up to a month.

BANANA BREAD

 Will

Skill > Advanced

Banana bread is sweet enough to be a delicious snack and healthy enough to be a breakfast treat. For breakfast, I like to add a slab of butter to the bread.

ACTIVE TIME: 15 minutes > **TOTAL TIME: 90 minutes** > **MAKES: 12 servings**

EQUIPMENT

Loaf pan

Medium mixing bowl

Fork

Large mixing bowl

Mixing spoon

Small mixing bowl

Whisk

Oven mitts

Wire rack

INGREDIENTS

4 tablespoons butter, plus more for greasing the loaf pan

3 ripe bananas

¾ cup sucanat (whole cane sugar)

2 eggs

½ cup milk

1 teaspoon vanilla

¾ teaspoon cinnamon

½ teaspoon ground nutmeg

1 teaspoon baking soda

½ teaspoon coarse sea salt

2 cups sprouted flour

1. Put an oven rack in the center of the oven and preheat the oven to 350°F. Grease a loaf pan thoroughly with butter.

2. In a medium bowl, using a fork, mash the bananas and set aside.

3. In a large bowl, add the butter and sucanat and mix with a mixing spoon until combined.

4. In a small bowl, add the eggs and milk, then whisk together until combined. Add the egg mixture to the butter mixture in the large bowl and stir to combine. Stir in the vanilla, cinnamon, nutmeg, baking soda, and sea salt until combined well. Add the flour and mashed bananas and stir until combined. Pour the batter into the prepared loaf pan.

5. Wearing oven mitts, put the loaf pan on the rack in the center of the oven and bake the bread for 45–50 minutes, or until a knife inserted into the center of the loaf comes out mostly clean.

6. Wearing oven mitts, transfer the hot loaf pan to a wire rack to cool.

BUFFALO WINGS

 Will

Who doesn't love a delicious mixture of spicy sauce and chicken you can eat with your fingers? Dig in!

ACTIVE TIME: 20 minutes > TOTAL TIME: 65–70 minute > MAKES: 6 servings

EQUIPMENT

Large wire rack

Large rimmed baking
   sheet

Small saucepan

Butter knife

Cutting board

Chef's knife

Large mixing bowl

Measuring spoons

Oven mitts

Whisk

Vegetable peeler

2 bowls for serving
   vegetables and
   dressing

Cooling rack

Tongs

1. Preheat the oven to 400°F. Set a large wire rack on a large rimmed baking sheet.

2. Put a small saucepan on top of a burner on the stove and turn the heat to low. With a butter knife, add the butter to the pan and let it melt. Turn off the heat and move the saucepan to a cool burner on the stove. Set aside.

3. Working on a cutting board and using a chef's knife, remove the tips of the chicken wings and discard. Cut apart the drumettes and the flats.

4. Transfer the wings to a large bowl, add the melted butter, sea salt, and black pepper, and toss with your hands to coat. Arrange the wings in a single layer on the prepared rack set on the baking sheet. Wash your hands and the bowl, cutting board, and knife. You do not have to clean the saucepan.

5. Wearing oven mitts, transfer the baking sheet to the oven, and bake the wings until cooked through and the skin is crispy, about 45–50 minutes.

6. Meanwhile, make the sauce. Put the small saucepan on a burner on the stove and turn the heat to low. With the butter knife, add the butter to the pan and let it melt. Transfer the butter to the clean large bowl, add the apple cider vinegar, chili powder, garlic powder, onion powder, sweet paprika, smoked paprika, pepper, sea salt, and cayenne pepper, and whisk until combined well. Set aside.

Ingredients

FOR THE WINGS

4½ tablespoons butter

6 pounds chicken wings

3 teaspoons coarse
sea salt

⅓ teaspoon ground
black pepper

FOR THE SAUCE

5 tablespoons butter

9 tablespoons apple cider
vinegar

1½ teaspoons chili powder

2 tablespoons garlic
powder

1½ teaspoons onion
powder

1½ teaspoons sweet
paprika

¾ teaspoon smoked
paprika

¾ teaspoon ground
black pepper

½ teaspoon coarse
sea salt

Cayenne pepper, to taste

FOR SERVING

9 carrots

9 stalks celery

Bottled blue cheese
dressing

7. Working on a clean cutting board and using a vegetable peeler, peel the carrots. With the cleaned chef's knife, cut the carrots into 4-inch sticks. Cut the celery stalks lengthwise, then cut into 4-inch sticks. Put the vegetables and blue cheese dressing into separate little bowls.

8. When the wings are cooked through and crispy, wearing oven mitts, carefully remove the cooked wings from the oven and transfer them, still on the rack and baking sheet, to a cooling rack. While the wings are still hot, transfer them to the large bowl of buffalo sauce with tongs. Toss the wings to coat in the sauce.

9. Serve the wings immediately with the carrot and celery sticks and the blue cheese dressing.

"CORNBREAD" MUFFINS

By Katie

Skill > Advanced

Lots of people love cornbread, but some never get to enjoy it because they are sensitive to wheat or corn. This recipe is delicious and satisfying like cornbread . . . without the corn!

ACTIVE TIME: 10 minutes > **TOTAL TIME:** 25–30 minutes > **MAKES:** 4 servings

EQUIPMENT

Standard 12-cup
 muffin tin

9 muffin/cupcake
 paper liners

Medium bowl

Measuring cups and
 spoons

Fork

Oven mitts

Toothpick for testing

INGREDIENTS

2½ cups almond flour

½ teaspoon baking soda

½ teaspoon sea salt

4 large eggs

1 tablespoon honey

1 tablespoon apple cider
 vinegar

2 tablespoons melted
 butter, coconut oil, or
 palm shortening

1. Preheat the oven to 350°F. Line a standard size muffin tin with 9 paper liners.

2. In a medium bowl, add the almond flour, baking soda, and sea salt and stir together with a fork to combine. Add the eggs, honey, vinegar, and butter and stir again until well combined.

3. Using a ¼ cup measuring cup, measure out level scoops of batter and place a scoop into each paper liner in the muffin tin. Smooth the top with your clean hands as you go.

4. Wearing oven mitts, place the muffin tin in the oven, and bake the muffins for 15–18 minutes, or until a toothpick comes out clean.

5. Wearing oven mitts, carefully transfer the hot muffin tin to a cool burner on the stove and let the muffins cool.

SERVING IDEAS

You can either slather these muffins with butter and a drizzle of syrup as a snack or make them into breakfast sandwiches with Turkey Breakfast Sausage on page 47. They're also amazing with homemade Strawberry–Chia Seed Jam (page 143) on top.

Blender Bread

 By Katie

Skill > Advanced

You probably think making bread is hard, right? A lot of the time it is, but this gluten-free bread is different! To make it, all you have to do is blend the ingredients, pour them into a baking dish, and bake. Voilà! Use this bread to make any kind of sandwich snack you'd like. I sometimes make PBJs using the Strawberry–Chia Seed Jam recipe on page 143.

ACTIVE TIME: 10 minutes > **TOTAL TIME: 45–50 minutes** > **MAKES: 5 servings**

Equipment

4½- by 8½-inch loaf pan
  (1½ quarts)

Parchment paper

Blender

Measuring cups and
  spoons

Fork

Rubber spatula or spoon

Oven mitts

Butter knife

Medium bowl

Potholder or wire
  cooling rack

1. Preheat the oven to 350°F. Grease a 1½-quart bread pan with the oil and line it on all sides with parchment paper.

2. Put a blender on the counter. Add the eggs, apple cider vinegar, oil, honey, and ¼ cup of water to the blender.

3. Add the flour, arrowroot powder, flaxseed meal, salt, and baking soda to a medium mixing bowl. Stir together with a fork until well combined.

4. Add the flour mixture to the blender. Place the top firmly on the blender and blend on high speed for 45–60 seconds.

5. Turn the blender off and pour the batter into the prepared bread pan. Use a rubber spatula or spoon if needed to scrape the batter from the blender into the pan.

6. Wearing oven mitts, place the bread pan in the hot oven and bake the bread for 35 minutes.

Ingredients

- ¼ teaspoon avocado, coconut, or olive oil (for greasing the bread pan)
- 4 large eggs
- 2 tablespoons apple cider vinegar
- 2 tablespoons avocado or olive oil
- 2 tablespoons honey
- ¼ cup water
- 1 cup almond flour
- ⅓ cup arrowroot powder
- ½ cup golden flaxseed meal
- ¼ teaspoon salt
- ½ teaspoon baking soda (level on the top)

7. After 35 minutes, test the bread. With a butter knife, pierce the middle of the loaf straight down halfway through the loaf. Pull the knife straight out again. If the knife is clean when you pull it out, the bread loaf is ready. If the knife comes out with batter sticking to the metal, put the pan back into the oven and let it bake another 3–5 minutes. Clean off the knife and check it again.

8. When the knife comes out clean, wearing oven mitts, transfer the hot loaf pan to a potholder or wire cooling rack. Allow the bread to cool for at least 20 minutes before removing the loaf from the pan.

Cinnamon Raisin Bread with Cream Cheese Glaze

By Katie

Skill > Advanced

My family doesn't eat a lot of sweets during the week, but on the weekends my mama usually lets me bake something special. This honey-sweetened bread with raisins and cinnamon is one of my favorite things to make. I like it without the cream cheese glaze, but my brothers like to spread a thick glaze on top. I suggest you try it both ways and decide for yourself!

ACTIVE TIME: 15 minutes > TOTAL TIME: 55–60 minutes > MAKES: 4 servings

Equipment

- 4½- by 8½-inch loaf pan (1½ quarts)
- Measuring cups and spoons
- Parchment paper
- Blender
- Medium mixing bowl
- Fork
- Rubber spatula or mixing spoon
- Oven mitts
- Butter knife
- Potholder or wire cooling rack
- Small bowl

1. Preheat the oven to 350°F. Grease a 1½-quart bread pan with the oil and line it on all sides with a piece of parchment paper.

2. Put a blender on the counter. Add the eggs, apple cider vinegar, avocado oil, honey, and 2 tablespoons of water to the blender.

3. Add the the flour, arrowroot powder, flaxseed meal, salt, baking soda, and cinnamon to a medium mixing bowl. Stir together with a fork until well combined.

4. Add the flour mixture to the blender. Place the top firmly on the blender and blend on high speed for 45–60 seconds.

5. Turn the blender off and remove the blender container from the base. Add the raisins and stir them into the mixture with a rubber spatula or mixing spoon.

6. Pour the batter into the prepared bread pan. Use a spatula or spoon if needed to scrape the batter out of the blender into the pan.

7. Wearing oven mitts, place the bread pan in the hot oven and bake the bread for 40 minutes.

Ingredients

FOR THE BREAD

¼ teaspoon avocado, coconut, or olive oil for greasing the bread pan

4 large eggs

2 tablespoons apple cider vinegar

2 tablespoons avocado oil

⅓ cup honey

2 tablespoons water

1 cup almond flour

⅓ cup arrowroot powder

½ cup golden flaxseed meal

¼ teaspoon salt

½ teaspoon baking soda

1½ teaspoons cinnamon

¾ cup raisins

FOR THE CREAM CHEESE GLAZE (OPTIONAL)

2 tablespoons cream cheese (softened to room temperature)

1 tablespoon maple syrup

8. After 40 minutes, test the bread. With a butter knife, pierce the middle of the loaf straight down halfway through the loaf. Pull the knife straight out again. If the knife is clean when you pull it out, the bread loaf is ready. If the knife comes out with batter sticking to the metal, put the pan back into the oven and let it bake another 5 minutes. Clean off the knife. After 5 minutes, check it again with the cleaned knife.

9. When the knife comes out clean, wearing oven mitts, transfer the hot loaf pan to a potholder or wire cooling rack.

10. Allow the bread to cool for at least 10 minutes before adding the glaze (if using) while the bread is still in the pan, and allow the pan to cool for at least 20 minutes before removing the bread from the pan.

11. To make the glaze (if using), place the cream cheese in a small bowl, then add 1 teaspoon of the maple syrup and stir until well combined. Add 1 teaspoon more of the maple syrup to the cream cheese and stir again until combined, then add the remaining 1 teaspoon and stir again.

12. Pour the glaze over the bread and spread it over the top with a butter knife.

KALE CHIPS

 Katie

Skill > Advanced

When you want something crunchy and healthy, these kale chips can't be beat! I like to make a batch to snack on before watching a movie or going on a hike.

ACTIVE TIME: 5 minutes > TOTAL TIME: 25 minute > MAKES: 3 servings

EQUIPMENT

Medium bowl
Measuring spoons
Large baking sheet
Oven mitts
Tongs

INGREDIENTS

1 large bunch kale
2 tablespoons avocado or olive oil
½–1 teaspoon sea salt

1. Preheat the oven to 300°F.

2. Tear the kale leaves away from the stem, then tear the leaves again into bite-size pieces. Put the kale leaves in a medium bowl.

3. Pour the oil over the kale and toss the leaves with your hands until all the kale is coated.

4. Arrange the kale leaves on a large baking sheet, making sure that they are not touching.

5. Sprinkle the kale with a thin layer of sea salt, beginning with ½ teaspoon and adding more, depending on the amount of kale in your bunch and how much salt you like on your chips.

6. Wearing oven mitts, put the baking sheet in the oven and bake the kale for 10 minutes.

7. Wearing oven mitts, transfer the baking sheet to a cool burner on the stove. Flip the kale leaves over with tongs, then return the baking sheet back to the oven. Bake the kale for 8 minutes more.

8. Wearing oven mitts, remove the baking sheet from the oven again and check to see if the kale chips are crispy. If they are, serve them immediately. If not, bake them in the oven for a few more minutes.

Easy, Cheesy Popcorn

By Abigail

Skill > Easy

Do you ever crave cheesy popcorn, but realize you don't have any in the house? With this recipe, you can whip some up in 15 minutes and get to crunching right away!

ACTIVE TIME: 10 minutes > **TOTAL TIME: 12 minutes** > **SERVES: 5**

Equipment

Paper bag

Measuring cups

Microwave oven

Small microwave-safe bowl (to melt the butter)

Large spoons (optional)

Ingredients

1 cup popcorn kernels

½ cup melted butter

¾ cup Parmesan cheese

Salt to taste

1. Place the popcorn kernels in a paper bag.

2. Securely fold over the open end of the bag so that the kernels won't spill out, and place the bag in the microwave. Turn the microwave on for 2 minutes. Check the bag after about 1½ minutes to see whether the kernels have already popped.

3. When all the kernels have popped, transfer the popcorn to a large bowl and let it cool slightly. In the small bowl, melt the butter in the microwave for 30 seconds. Pour it over the popcorn and mix it in with a couple of large spoons—or try tossing it with your hands, without making too much of a mess.

4. Sprinkle the Parmesan cheese into the large bowl, toss the popcorn again, and add salt to taste.

Desserts

Peanut Butter & Jelly Cups >>> 173

No-Bake Cookies >>> 175

Peanut Butter & Chocolate Mini Cups >>> 176

Strawberry Crumble >>> 177

Mug Brownies >>> 179

Pumpkin Pie >>> 180

Strawberry Cheesecake >>> 182

Peach Cobbler >>> 184

Chocolate Chip Blondies >>> 186

Chocolate Chip Cookies >>> 188

Peanut Butter & Jelly Cups

By Katie   **Skill** > Easy

Made with creamy, dreamy peanut butter and a sweet jam filling, these PBJ cups are a twist on the classic peanut butter and jelly sandwich. You can make them with the Strawberry–Chia Seed Jam on page 143 or your favorite jam.

ACTIVE TIME: 5 minutes > **TOTAL TIME: 35–45 minutes** > **MAKES: 16 cups, serving 4**

Equipment

Mini-cupcake tin (with 16 cups)

16 mini-cupcake paper liners

Medium saucepan

Measuring cup and spoons

Mixing spoon

Ingredients

¾ cup peanut butter

¼ cup refined coconut oil

3 tablespoons maple syrup

2 tablespoons plus 2 teaspoons strawberry chia seed, jam (or jam of choice)

1. Line a mini-cupcake tin (with 16 cups) with paper liners.

2. In a medium saucepan, add the peanut butter, coconut oil, and maple syrup and stir together.

3. Put the saucepan on a burner on the stove and turn the heat to low. Stir the peanut butter mixture until it is well combined, then transfer the pan to a cool burner or cooling rack.

4. Using a measuring spoon, drop 2 teaspoons of peanut butter mixture into each paper-lined cup.

5. Transfer the cupcake tin to the freezer and allow that layer to set for 15 minutes.

6. Remove the tin from the freezer. Add ½ teaspoon of jam to each cup, then top each cup with 1 teaspoon more of the peanut butter mixture.

7. Transfer the tin back to the freezer for 30 minutes, or until the filling is firm.

8. Remove the tin from the freezer and serve the cups in their wrappers. (You can store any leftover cups in the refrigerator.)

No-Bake Cookies

By Katie   **Skill** > Moderate

Crunchy and chocolatey, these easy no-bake cookies were the first recipe I ever created. My mom loves the way the kitchen smells when I make them, which is pretty often because no one ever seems to get tired of them. I hope you love them, too!

ACTIVE TIME: 10 minutes > **TOTAL TIME: 40–45 minutes** > **MAKES: 12 cookies**

Equipment

Parchment paper
Baking sheet
Food processor
Measuring cups and
    spoons
Large bowl
Mixing spoon
Small saucepan

Ingredients

⅓ cup walnuts

⅓ cup pecans

1 cup finely shredded
    unsweetened coconut
    flakes

⅓ cup sunflower seeds

⅓ cup honey

4½ teaspoons
    unsweetened cocoa
    powder

⅓ cup coconut butter

1 teaspoon vanilla extract

⅓ cup almond butter

1. Place a sheet of parchment paper on top of a baking sheet.

2. Put a food processor on the counter. Add the walnuts and pecans to the food processor and pulse 4 or 5 times until the nuts are cut into small or medium pieces.

3. In a large bowl, add the chopped nuts, coconut flakes, and sunflower seeds and, using a mixing spoon, stir to combine. Set aside.

4. Add the honey, cocoa powder, coconut butter, and vanilla extract to a small saucepan and stir to combine. Put the saucepan on a burner on the stove and turn the heat to medium-high. When the mixture starts to boil, turn off the heat and transfer the pan to a cool burner on the stove. Stir in the almond butter until combined, then immediately pour the mixture into the bowl with the nuts and coconut flakes and stir until the dough is well combined.

5. Using a measuring spoon, scoop 2 tablespoons of dough onto a work surface. Using your hands, roll the dough into a small ball, then place the ball on the prepared baking sheet. Form more balls in the same way, until all the dough has been used.

6. Transfer the baking sheet to the freezer and allow the cookies to chill and firm up for 30 minutes before serving. Store any remaining cookies in the refrigerator.

Peanut Butter & Chocolate Mini Cups

 Katie

Skill > Moderate

Perfectly peanut buttery and chocolatey, these tiny morsels are so tasty! They're adorable looking and super simple to make. I'd say the only challenge to this recipe is not eating them all at once.

ACTIVE TIME: 5 minutes > **TOTAL TIME: 35–40 minutes** > **MAKES: 3 servings**

Equipment

Mini-cupcake tin
  (with 16 cups)

9 mini-cupcake paper
  liners

Cutting board

Chef's knife

Measuring cups and
  spoons

Saucepan

Mixing spoon

Ingredients

¼ cup chocolate chunks
  or chocolate chips

⅓ cup peanut butter

¼ cup refined coconut oil

2 teaspoons maple syrup

1. Line 9 cups of a mini-cupcake tin with paper liners. If using the chocolate chunks, working on a cutting board and using a chef's knife, chop the chunks roughly into chocolate chip size and set aside. (If using chocolate chips, leave them whole.)

2. Put the peanut butter, coconut oil, and maple syrup in a saucepan. Put the pan on a burner on the stove and turn the heat to low, stirring with a mixing spoon until combined well. Turn off the heat and transfer the pan to a cool burner.

3. Using a measuring spoon, drop 1 tablespoon of the nut butter mixture into each lined mini cup, then top each cup with 1 rounded teaspoon of chocolate chunks.

4. Transfer the tin to the freezer for 30 minutes, or until the filling is firm.

5. After at least 30 minutes, pick up a mini cup by the wrapper and squeeze the wrapper very gently to see if the filling is solid. If it is, the cups are ready to eat; if not, put the tin back in the freezer and check again later.

STRAWBERRY CRUMBLE

By Will

Skill > Advanced

Strawberries are one of my favorite fruits to put in baked goods, and crumbles are my one of my favorite desserts!

ACTIVE TIME: 15 minutes > **TOTAL TIME: 45 minutes** > **MAKES: 6 servings**

EQUIPMENT

Cutting board

Paring knife

Citrus juicer

Large and medium mixing bowls

Mixing spoon

9- by 9-inch baking pan

Oven mitts

Cooling rack

INGREDIENTS

FOR THE FILLING

6 cups strawberries

1½ small lemons

4½ teaspoons tapioca starch

1 tablespoon vanilla extract

4½ teaspoons maple syrup

FOR THE CRUMBLE TOPPING

1½ cups almond flour

¾ teaspoon coarse sea salt

¼ cup coconut oil

¼ cup maple syrup

1. Preheat the oven to 350°F.

2. Working on a cutting board and using a paring knife, remove the leaves and stems from the strawberries and cut them in half. Cut the lemons in half. With a juicer, juice the lemons. In a large mixing bowl, add the strawberries, lemon juice, tapioca starch, vanilla, and maple syrup and stir gently with a mixing spoon to combine. Dump everything into a 9- by 9-inch baking pan and smooth out the top evenly with the back of the spoon.

3. Into a medium bowl, add the almond flour, sea salt, coconut oil, and maple syrup and stir to combine. Spread the mixture evenly over the strawberries in the baking pan.

4. Wearing oven mitts, transfer the baking pan to the hot oven and bake the crumble for 30 minutes, until the strawberries are juicy and bubbly and the topping is golden brown.

5. Wearing oven mitts, transfer the hot baking pan to a cooling rack. Let the crumble stand for 10 minutes before serving.

Mug Brownies

By Will

Skill > Moderate

Brownies are my favorite thing to bake and eat, so why not make healthier brownies in a mug? My question exactly, so here's the solution . . .

ACTIVE TIME: 5 minutes > **TOTAL TIME:** 30–35 minutes > **MAKES:** 6 servings

Equipment

Cutting board

Chef's knife

Large bowl

Measuring spoons

Mixing spoon

6 oven-safe mugs or
   ramekins

Rimmed baking sheet

Oven mitts

Cooling rack

Ingredients

12 ounces dark chocolate
   chunks or chocolate
   chips

¾ cup cashew butter

6 tablespoons honey

6 tablespoons apricot
   preserves
   (or use more honey)

¼ cup unsweetened cocoa
   powder

6 eggs

1½ teaspoons vanilla

¾ teaspoon coarse sea salt

¾ teaspoon baking soda

1. Preheat the oven to 350°F. If using chocolate chunks instead of chocolate chips, chop the chocolate into pieces, using a cutting board and chef's knife, and set them aside.

2. In a large bowl, add the cashew butter, honey, preserves, cocoa powder, salt, baking soda, eggs, and vanilla and stir with a mixing spoon until combined well.

3. Pour the batter into 6 oven-safe mugs or ramekins, dividing it equally. Sprinkle the tops with the chocolate pieces or chips. Put the mugs on a rimmed baking sheet.

4. Wearing oven mitts, transfer the baking sheet to the oven and bake the brownies for 25–30 minutes.

5. Wearing oven mitts, carefully remove the baking sheet from the oven and transfer the mugs to a large cooling rack. Let the brownies cool 5–10 minutes before serving.

6. Serve warm.

PUMPKIN PIE

 Anthony

Skill > Advanced

My mom always makes pumpkin pie around Thanksgiving, but it can be made any time of the year. This recipe has a lot of protein and healthy fats from the almond flour and eggs, and it doesn't have any refined sugar, so it can actually make a good breakfast too!

ACTIVE TIME: 15 minutes > **TOTAL TIME: 1 hour 15 minutes** > **MAKES: 6–8 servings**

EQUIPMENT

9-inch pie pan

Measuring cups and spoons

Medium bowl

Mixing spoon

Oven mitts

Spatula

Immersion blender or food processor

Cooling rack

Handheld mixer

Large bowl

1. Preheat the oven to 325°F. Lightly grease a 9-inch pie pan with coconut oil.

2. Prepare the pie shell. In a medium bowl, add the almond flour, cinnamon, egg, and coconut oil and stir with a mixing spoon until combined well and a dough forms. Press the dough into the bottom and up the sides of the prepared pie pan.

3. Wearing oven mitts, place the pie pan in the hot oven and bake the pie shell for 10–15 minutes, until it barely starts to brown.

4. Meanwhile, prepare the filling. In the same bowl (no need for extra dishes!) combine the pumpkin, eggs, honey, pumpkin pie spice, and vanilla. Using an immersion blender or food processor (a regular hand mixer will not get it as smooth), blend until smooth and spreadable (but not really pourable).

5. When the pie shell is done, wearing oven mitts, transfer the pie pan to a cooling rack. (Do not turn off the oven.) Spoon the filling into the shell and smooth the top with a spatula.

6. Wearing oven mitts, return the pan to the hot oven and bake the pie for 1 hour, or until the center is no longer jiggly. It will set more as it cools.

Ingredients

FOR THE PIE SHELL

3 tablespoons coconut oil, plus more to grease the pie pan

1 cup almond flour

¼–½ teaspoon cinnamon, or to taste

1 egg

FOR THE FILLING

1 (15-ounce) can pumpkin purée or 2 cups homemade puréed pumpkin with excess liquid drained

3 eggs

¼ cup honey or maple syrup, or to taste

1 tablespoon pumpkin pie spice (or combine 2 teaspoons cinnamon, ¼ teaspoon cloves, ¼ teaspoon ginger, and ¼ teaspoon nutmeg)

1 teaspoon vanilla extract

FOR THE TOPPING (OPTIONAL)

Coconut cream or heavy whipping cream

Chopped pecans

7. Wearing oven mitts, transfer the pie to a cooling rack and let cool completely.

8. Just before serving the pie, prepare the topping. With a handheld mixer in a large bowl, blend the coconut cream or heavy whipping cream until light and fluffy.

9. Serve the pie in slices with a dollop of whipped cream, or you can top the entire pie with the whipped cream, spreading it with a spatula to cover it completely. Sprinkle with some chopped pecans and serve.

STRAWBERRY CHEESECAKE

By Anthony

Skill > Advanced

Whenever you combine strawberries and cream cheese, it's impossible for it not to be good. This super creamy cheesecake is so easy to make. It's a great treat, especially in the summer, when locally grown strawberries are super sweet. We like to serve the cheesecake with fresh whipped cream.

ACTIVE TIME: 15 minutes > TOTAL TIME: 50 minutes > MAKES: 6–8 servings

EQUIPMENT

9-inch pie pan

Measuring cups and spoons

Medium bowl

Mixing spoon

Oven mitts

Handheld mixer or immersion blender

Cooling rack

Plastic wrap

Cutting board

Paring knife

1. Preheat the oven to 325°F. Lightly grease a 9-inch pie pan with coconut oil.

2. Prepare the pie shell. In a medium bowl, add the almond flour, cinnamon, egg, and coconut oil and stir together with a mixing spoon until a dough forms. Press the dough into the bottom and up the sides of the prepared pie pan.

3. Wearing oven mitts, place the pan in the hot oven and bake the pie shell for 10–15 minutes, until it barely starts to brown.

4. Meanwhile, prepare the filling. In the same bowl (no need for extra dishes!), combine the cream cheese, maple syrup, eggs, and vanilla. With a handheld mixer or an immersion blender, blend until smooth.

5. When the shell is done, wearing oven mitts, remove the pie shell from the oven and transfer to a cooling rack to cool slightly. (Do not turn the oven off.)

6. Pour the filling into the pie shell. Wearing oven mitts, place the pie pan back in the oven and bake the cheesecake for 35 minutes.

7. Wearing oven mitts, transfer the cheesecake to a cooling rack and let cool to room temperature.

INGREDIENTS

FOR THE PIE SHELL

3 tablespoons coconut oil, plus more to grease the pie pan

1 cup almond flour

¼–½ teaspoon cinnamon, or to taste

1 egg

FOR THE FILLING

2 (8-ounce) packages cream cheese, softened

¼ cup maple syrup

3 eggs

1 teaspoon fresh vanilla

FOR THE TOPPING

1 pound fresh strawberries

8. Cover the cooled cheesecake with plastic wrap. Transfer to the refrigerator and chill at least 4 hours or overnight before serving.

9. Just before serving, working on a cutting board and using a paring knife, remove the leaves and stems from the strawberries and cut them into ¼-inch slices. Arrange them in a pretty circular pattern on the top of the cheesecake and serve.

PEACH COBBLER

By Anthony   Skill > Advanced

Peaches are one of my favorite fruits, and this is one of my favorite ways to eat them. Try to make this cobbler in the summer when peaches are in season, but you can also use frozen peaches and make it any time of year (see the box on the next page).

ACTIVE TIME: 15 minutes > TOTAL TIME: 40 minutes > MAKES: 8 servings

EQUIPMENT

9- by 13-inch baking dish

Measuring cups and
    spoons

Medium bowl

Whisk

Oven mitts

Rubber scraper

Cutting board

Paring knife

1. Put the butter in a 9- by 13-inch baking dish and place the dish in the oven. Preheat the oven to 375°F.

2. While the butter melts in the oven, add the flour, sugar, baking powder, and salt to a medium bowl and whisk together. Add the milk and vanilla and whisk until the batter is just mixed.

3. When the butter is completely melted, put on oven mitts and carefully transfer the baking dish to a cool burner on the stove. Pour the batter over the butter. Use a rubber scraper to get all of the batter out of the bowl.

4. Working on a cutting board and using a paring knife, cut the peaches into slices and place them on top of the batter. Sprinkle the top with a tiny bit more sugar or some cinnamon, if desired.

5. Wearing oven mitts, place the baking dish in the hot oven and bake for 25 minutes, or until the fruit is cooked through.

6. Serve warm with whipped cream or ice cream if preferred.

INGREDIENTS

- 8 tablespoons (1 stick) butter
- 1 cup flour (see wheat flour substitutes on page 23)
- 1 cup organic sugar (or maple syrup and ¼ cup extra of flour), plus more for sprinkling over the batter, if desired
- 1 tablespoon baking powder
- ½ teaspoon salt
- 1 cup milk
- 1 teaspoon vanilla
- 3 pounds fresh peaches (8–9 large peaches)
- Cinnamon for sprinkling the batter, if desired

MAKE YEAR-ROUND

Although this cobbler is best when made with fresh, in-season peaches, you can make it anytime with frozen peaches, just be sure to let them defrost first or the topping will cook too much.

CHOCOLATE CHIP BLONDIES

By Katie

Skill > Moderate

These gooey, chocolaty blondies are the perfect dessert! You can serve them warm, or freeze them and enjoy them at another time. They make amazing chocolate blondie bites. They're so yummy they will stand out at any event.

PREP TIME: 15 minutes > **COOK TIME: 20–25 minutes** > **TOTAL TIME: 35–40 minutes** > **MAKES: 16**

EQUIPMENT

8- by 8-inch square pan
Piece parchment paper
Medium bowl
Measuring spoon set
Measuring cup (8 ounce)
Mixing spoon
Fork
Spatula
Oven mitts
Hot pad (or trivet)

INGREDIENTS

¼ cup oil plus ¼ teaspoon for oiling the pan
3 large eggs
¾ cup tahini
¾ cup coconut sugar
1½ teaspoons vanilla
1¼ cups almond flour
½ cup coconut flour
1 teaspoon baking powder
⅛ teaspoon salt
1 cup chocolate chips

1. Preheat the oven to 350°F.

2. Pour ¼ teaspoon of the oil into an 8- by 8-inch pan and grease it thoroughly. Line the pan with the parchment paper.

3. In a medium bowl, mix together the eggs, tahini, coconut oil, coconut sugar, and vanilla extract with a fork.

4. Add the almond flour, coconut flour, baking powder, and salt to the wet ingredients in the bowl and stir the mixture with a fork until all the ingredients are well combined.

5. Add the chocolate chips to the bowl and stir until the chips are evenly distributed in the batter.

6. Scoop the batter into the prepared pan and smooth out the top with a spatula. Bake for 20–25 minutes. You'll know the blondies are ready when the edges are slightly browned and a toothpick inserted in the middle of the pan comes out clean. If you get chocolate on your toothpick, try another spot. (It's super-melty and will coat the toothpick evenly when the blondies are done.)

7. When the blondies are done, remove the pan from the oven with oven mitts and place the pan on a trivet or hot pad on the kitchen counter (to protect the surface from getting damaged by the hot pan).

8. Let the pan cool for at least 30 minutes, and then remove the blondies from the pan, using the edges of parchment paper to lift them out.

9. Cut the blondies into pieces. If they are still warm, be careful as you pull them apart or they will break into pieces. They'll still be delicious, though!

CHOCOLATE CHIP COOKIES

By Abigail   **Skill** > Moderate

These cookies are a taste of heaven on earth. Their crumbly sugar cookie texture and perfectly balanced sweetness win over everybody who tries them. (My friends can vouch for that.) Also, the next time you need to ask your mom for something, be sure to whip up a batch of these cookies. You'll thank me.

ACTIVE TIME: 15 minutes > **TOTAL TIME:** 30 minutes > **MAKES:** about 1 dozen cookies

EQUIPMENT

Large mixing bowl
Baking sheet
Measuring cups and spoons
Mixing spoon
Large baking sheet
Parchment paper
Oven mitt
Fork

INGREDIENTS

2 cups all-purpose flour
½ teaspoon baking soda
½ teaspoon salt
1 large egg
½ cup melted butter
½ cup honey
2 teaspoons vanilla extract
1 cup semi-sweet chocolate chips

1. Preheat the oven to 350 F.

2. In a large bowl, mix together the flour, baking soda, and salt. Make sure there are no lumps in this dry mixture before adding the wet ingredients.

3. Add the egg to the dry ingredients in the bowl, mixing it in until there are no lumps. Add the butter, honey, and vanilla, and stir well.

4. Add the chocolate chips and stir until all the ingredients are well combined.

5. Line a baking sheet with parchment paper.

6. Use a tablespoon to scoop up some of the dough. Using your hands, roll the dough into small balls and place them onto the parchment paper. Do not flatten the balls of dough.

7. Carefully place the baking sheet in the oven. Set the timer for 7 minutes.

8. After the time is up, remove the baking sheet from the oven with an oven mitt and transfer it to the stovetop. Use a fork to squish down each of the cookies—just enough to change the shape from a circle to a squished oval. Be careful not to make the cookies crumble by flattening them too much.

9. Put the cookies back in the oven and bake them for another 5 minutes.

10. When the cookies are done, remove the baking sheet and let the cookies cool on the pan for about 15 minutes (or eat them right away!).

Surf Smoothie

By Will

Skill > Easy

I love tropical smoothies, especially ones based on mango. This tangy mango smoothie hits the tastes buds just right. It's one of my favorites, and it will probably become one of yours, too.

ACTIVE TIME: 10 minutes > **TOTAL TIME: 10 minutes** > **MAKES: 6 servings**

Equipment

Blender
Cutting board
Paring knife
Citrus juicer
Measuring cups

Ingredients

2 limes (1 lime half reserved for another recipe)

3 ripe mangos

1½ cups frozen mango pieces

¾ cup yogurt

1½ cups orange juice

1. Put a blender on the counter. Working on a cutting board and using a paring knife, cut the limes into halves and reserve one of the halves for another recipe. Using a citrus juicer, juice the three lime halves and add the juice to the blender. Remove and discard the skin of the fresh mangoes, cut the flesh into medium chunks, and add to the blender.

2. Add the frozen mango pieces, yogurt, and orange juice to the blender. Put the lid on tightly and blend for 2–3 minutes on high until smooth.

3. Serve immediately.

Funky Monkey Smoothie

By Will   **Skill** > Easy

I love everything about smoothies. I love making them, serving them, and most of all, I *love* drinking them. This smoothie really emphasizes the word *chocolate* in a completely new kind of way.

ACTIVE TIME: 10 minutes > **TOTAL TIME:** 10 minutes > **MAKES:** 4 servings

Equipment

Cutting board

Butter knife

Plastic container or freezer bag

Blender

Measuring cups and spoons

Ingredients

3 bananas

12 ounces canned full-fat coconut milk

¼ cup almond butter, or any nut butter of your choice

3 tablespoons unsweetened cocoa powder

2 tablespoons maple syrup

1. The day before serving the smoothie, prepare and freeze the bananas. Working on a cutting board and using a butter knife, peel the banana and cut the flesh into rounds. Put the rounds in a plastic container or freezer bag and transfer them to the freezer until frozen, overnight. (Alternatively, you can use fresh bananas and add ice when blending.)

2. Put a blender on the counter. Add the frozen bananas (or fresh bananas and ice), coconut milk, almond butter, cocoa powder, and maple syrup to the blender. Put the lid on tightly and blend everything together.

3. Serve immediately.

STRAWBERRY-MINT SMOOTHIE

By Katie

By Katie

Skill > Easy

Last summer I began training to become a lifeguard, and after a hot morning in the sun, my mom would take me to our local smoothie shop to cool down. This smoothie is a recreation of one of my favorite drinks on the menu. It's so refreshing!

ACTIVE TIME: 5 minutes > TOTAL TIME: 5 minutes > MAKES: 2 servings

EQUIPMENT

Blender

Measuring cups and
    spoons

Spoon

INGREDIENTS

2 cups frozen strawberries

2 tablespoons maple
    syrup or honey, plus
    more if needed

⅛ teaspoon peppermint
    extract

1 cup water

1. Put a blender on the counter. Add the strawberries, maple syrup, peppermint extract, and water to the blender. Put the lid on tightly and blend until smooth.

2. Turn the blender off. Remove the lid and taste a small amount with a spoon. Add additional maple syrup or honey, if needed.

3. Serve immediately.

ICE POP IDEA

If you'd like to make this recipe into ice pops, pour the mixture into an ice pop mold and put in the freezer overnight before serving.

Fall Smoothie

By Paul

Suddenly, one day last fall, I felt inspired to make a smoothie. I have no idea why, but man, this turned out way better than I expected. With the pumpkin and maple syrup, it just tastes like autumn.

ACTIVE TIME: 10 minutes > **TOTAL TIME:** 10 minutes > **MAKES:** about 5 servings

Equipment

Blender

Measuring cups and spoons

Can opener

Ingredients

1 cup milk

½ cup unsweetened applesauce

3–4 ice cubes

1 teaspoon maple syrup

¼ teaspoon cinnamon

⅛ teaspoon ginger

¼–½ cup canned pumpkin, to taste (¼ cup lets the spices come through and blend with the pumpkin taste; ½ cup makes it taste very strongly of pumpkin)

1. Put a blender on the counter and add the milk, applesauce, ice, maple syrup, cinnamon, and ginger to the blender. Using the can opener, open the can of pumpkin and add as much as you like to the blender. Put the lid on tightly and blend for 10–15 seconds on high speed if you have a low-power blender, or on low speed if you have a high-power blender, until you stop hearing the ice rattle around inside.

2. Check the mixture. When the smoothie is uniform (everything looks the same), it is ready to serve. This smoothie keeps in the refrigerator for a day or two.

HOMEMADE HOT COCOA

By Anthony

Skill > Moderate

Did you know that chocolate has a lot of flavonoids, which are antioxidants? This means that when it isn't packed with sugar, cocoa can be really good for us. It's also just delicious, of course, and this is one way to drink it without too much added sweetness.

ACTIVE TIME: 10 minutes > TOTAL TIME: 10 minutes > MAKES: 4 servings

EQUIPMENT

Medium saucepan

Measuring cups and spoons

Whisk

4 mugs

INGREDIENTS

4 cups milk of choice (cow's milk, almond milk, macadamia milk, oat milk or coconut milk)

½ cup cocoa powder

¼ cup maple syrup, or to taste (¼ cup makes a semisweet cocoa)

1 teaspoon vanilla extract

Tiny pinch of salt

1. In a medium saucepan, add ½ cup of the milk, cocoa powder, maple syrup, vanilla, and salt, and whisk together until combined.

2. Put the saucepan on a burner on the stove and set the heat to medium. Whisk for 2 minutes more, then add the remaining 3½ cups milk and whisk to combine well. Continue to cook, whisking, until hot.

3. Serve immediately in 4 mugs.

Tip

For an even smoother hot cocoa, use an immersion blender to blend everything together in the saucepan.

HEALTHY "FRUIT PUNCH"

By Will

Skill > Moderate

I am not someone who is into teas, so it may surprise you that I *love* hibiscus tea. It really tastes like a punch, and so it is often served as a punch.

ACTIVE TIME: 10 minutes > **TOTAL TIME: 10 minutes** > **MAKES: 4 servings**

EQUIPMENT

Measuring cups and spoons

Medium saucepan

Serving pitcher

INGREDIENTS

1 quart filtered cool water

¼ cups dried hibiscus flowers

2 tablespoons honey

1. Put 2 cups of the filtered water into a medium saucepan.

2. Put the saucepan of water on a burner on the stove and turn the heat to high. Bring the water to a boil, then add the dried hibiscus flowers and turn off the heat. Allow the flowers to steep until the liquid is dark red.

3. Add the remaining 2 cups of cool water to the hibiscus liquid and stir to combine. Add the raw honey, stirring until well combined.

4. Pour the tea into a serving pitcher and serve in tall glasses filled with ice.

Meal Planning Like a Pro

WRITTEN BY WILL

Any kind of planning takes a bit of time and energy, and planning out meals for the week so you'll know exactly what you are going to be having to eat each day is no exception. If you are thinking *Why would I have to do that?*, you're not alone. The first time I heard of meal planning, I wondered the same thing. Surprisingly, it makes your life a lot easier. When you are in charge of cooking one, two, or all three meals a day without a plan, it can get hectic. You can end up with too much of one ingredient, not enough of others, and too many random foods going bad in your fridge. Meal planning is your ticket out of that chaos, and you can eat healthier, save time, save money, and even save the environment. Let me explain.

When life gets busy, we often turn to hunting around in the refrigerator for something to eat and end up making a PB&J for dinner, or we might even end up ordering fast food. Needless to say, while this is okay once in a while, it is not ideal if you want to eat nutritional, balanced healthy meals. You can avoid all this by planning meals in advance.

Once you are prepared, with all the ingredients you will need, you will actually save time. No more arguments with your family about what's for dinner,

either! And then there is the money-saving aspect of planning ahead. Have you ever seen your parents' grocery receipt? Food is expensive, and cutting down on the things you don't need can really make a difference with the family budget. On a broader scale, did you know that 38 million tons of food are wasted every year in the United States alone? When you think about all the land and water that goes into making that much food, you can see how big of a problem waste is! Meal planning helps to reduce this problem.

HOW TO MEAL PLAN

Now that you understand why you should meal plan, let's discuss how you can go about it. Well, there are three main methods: leftovers, batch cooking, and quick and easy cooking.

First, let's talk about leftovers—and by leftovers, I don't just mean eating the cold food that you didn't finish from your last meal. Instead, the idea is to cook something substantial, like a roast chicken, that can be used throughout the week in various ways. For example, if you roast a chicken or two (depending on the size of your family) on a Saturday, you can use the bones to make chicken broth on Sunday, and then use the meat to make soups, tacos, salads, and sandwiches for the next few days. So you only have to cook chicken once, but you will be reaping its rewards for days.

You can also batch cook. Batch cooking is where you cook all your food for the week over the course of a day or two, so throughout the week you won't have to worry about what's for dinner. You just have to heat up your meals when you're ready to eat. For example, you could make pancakes, steak, soup, and a casserole all in one day and use them all week. You just have to store them correctly so everything stays nice and fresh.

Last, you can plan for quick and easy meals. This is when you just cook something simple at meal times that won't necessarily have leftovers. For example, on Fridays, you might just make burgers or pizza.

To get you started, below is a sample meal plan for a week of dinners to be made by kids with adult supervision. All the recipes are from this cookbook, so if you have other favorites, feel free to make any substitutions. The idea here is to get us involved with both the planning and the cooking of our family meals.

Sample Meal Plan: A Week of Family Dinners

SATURDAY:
- Make the Turkey Chili (page 102) and put it in the refrigerator to serve on Monday night.
- Make the Taco Casserole (page 82) for dinner tonight.

SUNDAY:
- Make the Cheesy Beef, Potato, & Carrot Casserole (page 133) and put it in the refrigerator to serve on Wednesday night.
- Make the Grilled Cheese (page 114) for a light dinner tonight.

MONDAY:
- Heat and serve the Turkey Chili (page 102) you made on the weekend.

TUESDAY:
- Make something quick and easy, like the Maple-Glazed Chicken Thighs (page 98) and a steamed vegetable.

WEDNESDAY:
- Heat and serve the Cheesy Beef, Potato, & Carrot Casserole (page 133) you made on the weekend along with a green salad.

THURSDAY:
- Make something quick and easy, like the Garden-Fresh Pesto Pasta (page 109).

FRIDAY:
- Make something quick and easy, like the Fish Tacos (page 128).

METRIC CONVERSION CHARTS

* The recipes that appear in this cookbook use the standard United States method for measuring liquid and dry or solid ingredients (teaspoons, tablespoons, and cups). The information on this chart is provided to help cooks outside the U.S. successfully use these recipes. All equivalents are approximate.

METRIC EQUIVALENTS FOR DIFFERENT TYPES OF INGREDIENTS

STANDARD CUP	FINE POWDER (e.g. flour)	GRAIN (e.g. rice)	GRANULAR (e.g. sugar)	LIQUID SOLIDS (e.g. butter)	LIQUID (e.g. milk)
¾	105 g	113 g	143 g	150 g	180 ml
⅔	93 g	100 g	125 g	133 g	160 ml
½	70 g	75 g	95 g	100 g	120 ml
⅓	47 g	50 g	63 g	67 g	80 ml
¼	35 g	38 g	48 g	50 g	60 ml
⅛	18 g	19 g	24 g	25 g	30 ml

USEFUL EQUIVALENTS FOR LIQUID INGREDIENTS BY VOLUME

¼ tsp	=					1 ml
½ tsp	=					2 ml
1 tsp	=					5 ml
3 tsp	=	1 tbls	=	½ fl oz	=	15 ml
		2 tbls	=	⅛ cup	=	1 fl oz	=	30 ml
		4 tbls	=	¼ cup	=	2 fl oz	=	60 ml
		5⅓ tbls	=	⅓ cup	=	3 fl oz	=	80 ml
		8 tbls	=	½ cup	=	4 fl oz	=	120 ml
		10⅔ tbls	=	⅔ cup	=	5 fl oz	=	160 ml
		12 tbls	=	¾ cup	=	6 fl oz	=	180 ml
		16 tbls	=	1 cup	=	8 fl oz	=	240 ml
		1 pt	=	2 cups	=	16 fl oz	=	480 ml
		1 qt	=	4 cups	=	32 fl oz	=	960 ml
					33 fl oz	=	1000 ml= 1 L

USEFUL EQUIVALENTS FOR DRY INGREDIENTS BY WEIGHT

(To convert ounces to grams, multiply the number of ounces by 30.)

1 oz	=	⅟₁₆ lb	=	30 g
4 oz	=	¼ lb	=	120 g
8 oz	=	½ lb	=	240 g
12 oz	=	¾ lb	=	360 g
16 oz	=	1 lb	=	480 g

USEFUL EQUIVALENTS FOR COOKING/OVEN TEMPERATURES

	Fahrenheit	Celsius	Gas Mark
Freeze Water	32° F	0° C	
Room Temperature	68° F	20° C	
Boil Water	212° F	100° C	
Bake	325° F	160° C	3
	350° F	180° C	4
	375° F	190° C	5
	400° F	200° C	6
	425° F	220° C	7
	450° F	230° C	8
Broil			Grill

USEFUL EQUIVALENTS LENGTH

(To convert inches to centimeters, multiply the number of inches by 2.5.)

1 in	=					2.5 cm	
6 in	=	½ ft	=			15 cm	
12 in	=	1 ft	=			30 cm	
36 in	=	3 ft	=	1 yd	=	90 cm	
40 in	=					100 cm	= 1 m

INDEX

Note: Page numbers in *italics* indicate photos separate from recipe text.

A

Abigail. *See* Langford, Abigail

Agar, as egg substitute, 22

Anthony. *See* Spears, Anthony

Apples
  about: applesauce as egg
    substitute, 21
  Apple Sandwiches, 54–55

Apricot Preserves, 38–39

Apricots, in Trail Mix, 139

Arrowroot starch, about, 23

Avocados
  about: cutting, peeling, slicing,
    scooping out, 60
  Avocado Chicken Salad, 60–61
  Avocado Quesadilla, 66–67
  BLTA Sandwich, 64
  Easy Chicken Avocado Soup,
    70–71
  Guacamole, *148–149*
  Taco Salad, 62–63

B

Bacon
  about: as soup addition, 107
  Apple Sandwiches, 54–55
  Bacon Tomato Soup, 68–69
  Bacon-Wrapped Dates, 140–141
  BLTA Sandwich, 64
  Oven-Baked Eggs & Bacon, 40

Baked Fish Sticks with Tartar Sauce,
    90–91

Baked Oatmeal Squares, *42–43*

Baking sheet (rimmed), 46

Bananas
  about: as egg substitutes, 22
  Banana Bread, *158–159*
  Blueberry-Banana Ice Pops, 144
  Funky Monkey Smoothie, *194–195*
  Monkey Salad, 147
  Plantain Chips, 150

Bartlett, Will
  about, 7
  Avocado Chicken Salad, 60–61
  Avocado Quesadilla, 66–67
  Bacon Tomato Soup, 68–69
  Banana Bread, *158–159*
  BLTA Sandwich, 64
  Breakfast Burritos, 36–37
  Buffalo Wings, 160–161
  Coconut Chicken Nuggets, 124–125
  Crêpes, 38–39
  Easy Chicken Avocado Soup,
    70–71
  Fish Tacos, 128–129
  Funky Monkey Smoothie, *194–195*
  Healthy "Fruit Punch," 199
  Kid-Friendly Broccoli, 113
  Lime-Marinated Steak, 126–127
  Mac 'n' Cheese, *58–59*
  Mug Brownies, *178–179*
  Plantain Chips, 150
  School Day Blueberry Pancakes,
    34–35

Simple Mashed Potatoes, 100

Strawberry Crumble, 177

Surf Smoothie, 193

Taco Salad, 62–63

Beans and lentils
  Black Bean Soup, 72–73
  Lentil Soup, 56–57
  Oven-Roasted Green Beans,
    120–121
  Pinto Gallo (Gallo Pinto), 116–117

Beef
  about: buying, 11, 11–12; grocery
    store label definitions (organic,
    natural, grass-fed), 11
  Best Burger with Secret Yum
    Sauce, 92–93
  Cheeseburger Casserole, 80–81
  Cheeseburger Soup, 106–107
  Cheesy Beef, Potato, & Carrot
    Casserole, 133–135
  Garlic Beef Jerky, 156–157
  Great-Grandma's Spaghetti from
    Italy, *110–112*
  Lime-Marinated Steak, 126–127
  Taco Casserole, 82–83
  Taco Salad, 62–63

Berries
  about: blueberries, 26
  Baked Oatmeal Squares, *42–43*
  Berry Yogurt Ice Pops, 146
  Blueberry-Banana Ice Pops, 144
  Chia Pudding, *26–27*

Berries (continued)
School Day Blueberry Pancakes, 34–35
Strawberry Cheesecake, 182–183
Strawberry–Chia Seed Jam, 142–143
Strawberry Crumble, 177
Strawberry-Mint Smoothie, 196
Strawberry-Pecan Salad, 52–53
Best Burger with Secret Yum Sauce, 92–93
Black Bean Soup, 72–73
Blender Bread, 164–165
Blenders, using, 14–15, 105
Blondies, chocolate chip, 186–187
Bread
Banana Bread, 158–159
Blender Bread, 164–165
Cinnamon Raisin Bread with Cream Cheese Glaze, 166–167
"Cornbread" Muffins, 162–163
Breakfast, 25–47
Baked Oatmeal Squares, 42–43
Breakfast Burritos, 36–37
Breakfast Casserole, 45
Chia Pudding, 26–27
Crêpes, 38–39
Flourless Banana Split Pancakes, 30–31
Oven-Baked Eggs & Bacon, 40
Oven Pancake, 41
School Day Blueberry Pancakes, 34–35
Scrambled Eggs, 28–29
Texas-Style Breakfast Tacos, 44
Tiramisu French Toast, 32–33
Turkey Breakfast Sausage, 46–47
Breakfast Casserole, 45
Broccoli
Fried Broccoli & Cauliflower, 96
Kid-Friendly Broccoli, 113
Brownies, mug, 178–179
Buffalo Wings, 160–161
Burritos, 36–37
Buying food, 10–12

C
Cage-free, defined, 11–12
Caramel Carrots, 101
Carrots
Caramel Carrots, 101
Cheesy Beef, Potato, & Carrot Casserole, 133–135
Cauliflower
Creamed Cauliflower, 74–75
Fried Broccoli & Cauliflower, 96
Pizza Cauliflower Soup, 104–105
Cheese
about: best for grilled cheese sandwiches, 115
Avocado Quesadilla, 66–67
Breakfast Casserole, 45
Cheeseburger Casserole, 80–81
Cheeseburger Soup, 106–107
Cheesy Beef, Potato, & Carrot Casserole, 133–135
Cream Cheese Glaze, 167
Margherita Pizza, 85–87
Mascarpone Cream, 32
pasta with. See Pasta
sandwiches/wraps with. See Sandwiches and wraps
Strawberry Cheesecake, 182–183
Taco Casserole, 82–83
Taco Cheese Sauce, 152–153
Tomato, Zucchini, & Mozzarella Bake, 84
Chia Pudding, 26–27
Chicken
about: buying, 11–12; grocery store label definitions (organic, natural, grass-fed, pasture raised, cage-free), 11–12
Avocado Chicken Salad, 60–61
Buffalo Wings, 160–161
Chicken Broth, 97
Chicken Ranch Wraps with Greek Yogurt Ranch Dressing, 88–89
Coconut Chicken Nuggets, 124–125
Easy Chicken Avocado Soup, 70–71

Honey-Mustard Chicken, 132
Mediterranean Sun-Dried Tomato Chicken, 130–131
Super-Quick Gravy, 99
Chocolate
Chocolate Chip Blondies, 186–187
Chocolate Chip Cookies, 188–189
Funky Monkey Smoothie, 194–195
Homemade Hot Cocoa, 198
Mug Brownies, 178–179
No-Bake Cookies, 174–175
Peanut Butter & Chocolate Mini Cups, 176
Tiramisu French Toast, 32–33
White Hot Chocolate, 151
Cinnamon Raisin Bread with Cream Cheese Glaze, 166–167
Citrus
Mango Lemonade, 192
Pineapple-Lemon Ice Pops, 145
Surf Smoothie, 193
Clean Fifteen, 11
Cobbler, peach, 184–185
Coconut
Coconut Chicken Nuggets, 124–125
Gluten-Free Puffy Snack Mix, 138
Maple Granola, 154–155
Monkey Salad, 147
Trail Mix, 139
Coconut flour, about, 23
Corn
about: substitutes, 22
Easy, Cheesy Popcorn, 169
"Cornbread" Muffins, 162–163
Cream Cheese Glaze, 167
Creamed Cauliflower, 74–75
Crêpes, 38–39
Crispy, Crunchy Potatoes, 118–119
Cucumber Salad, 50–51

D
Dairy. See also Yogurt
buying, 11–12
substitutes, 20–21

Dates, bacon-wrapped, 140–141
Dehydrators, using, 16, 154
Desserts, 171–189. *See also* Snacks
    Chocolate Chip Blondies, 186–187
    Chocolate Chip Cookies, 188–189
    Mug Brownies, *178–179*
    No-Bake Cookies, *174–175*
    Peach Cobbler, 184–185
    Peanut Butter & Chocolate Mini
        Cups, 176
    Peanut Butter & Jelly Cups, *172–173*
    Pumpkin Pie, 180–181
    Strawberry Cheesecake, 182–183
    Strawberry Crumble, 177
Dessinger, Katie
    about, 9
    Apple Sandwiches, *54–55*
    Blender Bread, 164–165
    Chocolate Chip Blondies, 186–187
    Cinnamon Raisin Bread with
        Cream Cheese Glaze, 166–167
    "Cornbread" Muffins, *162–163*
    Honey-Mustard Chicken, 132
    Kale Chips, 168
    Maple Granola, 154–155
    Mediterranean Sun-Dried Tomato
        Chicken, *130–131*
    No-Bake Cookies, *174–175*
    Peanut Butter & Chocolate Mini
        Cups, 176
    Peanut Butter & Jelly Cups,
        172–173
    Strawberry–Chia Seed Jam,
        142–143
    Strawberry-Mint Smoothie, 196
    Tomato, Zucchini, & Mozzarella
        Bake, 84
    Turkey Breakfast Sausage, *46–47*
    Turkey Chili, 102–103
    White Hot Chocolate, 151
Dinner, 95–135
    Caramel Carrots, 101
    Cheeseburger Soup, 106–107
    Cheesy Beef, Potato, & Carrot
        Casserole, 133–135

Chicken Broth, 97
Coconut Chicken Nuggets,
    124–125
Crispy, Crunchy Potatoes, *118–119*
Fish Tacos, 128–129
Fried Broccoli & Cauliflower, 96
Garden-Fresh Pesto Pasta,
    108–109
Great-Grandma's Spaghetti from
    Italy, *110–112*
Grilled Cheese, 114–115
Honey-Mustard Chicken, 132
Kid-Friendly Broccoli, 113
Lime-Marinated Steak, 126–127
Maple-Glazed Chicken Thighs, 98
Mediterranean Sun-Dried Tomato
    Chicken, *130–131*
Oven-Baked Sweet Potato Fries,
    122–123
Oven-Roasted Green Beans,
    120–121
Pinto Gallo (Gallo Pinto), 116–117
Pizza Cauliflower Soup, 104–105
Simple Mashed Potatoes, 100
Super-Quick Gravy, 99
Turkey Chili, 102–103
Dirty Dozen, 10–11
Drinks, 191–199
    Fall Smoothie, 197
    Funky Monkey Smoothie, *194–195*
    Healthy "Fruit Punch," 199
    Homemade Hot Cocoa, 198
    Mango Lemonade, 192
    Strawberry-Mint Smoothie, 196
    Surf Smoothie, 193
    White Hot Chocolate, 151

E

Easy, Cheesy Popcorn, 169
Easy Chicken Avocado Soup, 70–71
Eggs
    about: buying, 11–12; cracking, 40;
        separating, 29; substitutes,
        21–22
    Breakfast Casserole, 45

Crêpes, 38–39
Egg Drop Soup, *76–77*
Egg Fried Rice, 78–79
Oven-Baked Eggs & Bacon, 40
Scrambled Eggs, 28–29
Texas-Style Breakfast Tacos, 44
Tiramisu French Toast, 32–33
Equipment. *See* Kitchen equipment,
    use and safety; *specific recipes*

F

Fall Smoothie, 197
Fish and seafood
    about: buying, 12
    Baked Fish Sticks with Tartar
        Sauce, 90–91
    Fish Tacos, 128–129
Flourless Banana Split Pancakes, *30–31*
Flour, wheat substitutes, 23
Free-range, defined, 12
French toast, 32–33
Fried Broccoli & Cauliflower, 96
Fruit. *See also specific fruit*
    about: buying, 10–11
    Healthy "Fruit Punch," 199
Funky Monkey Smoothie, *194–195*

G

Garden-Fresh Pesto Pasta, *108–109*
Garlic Beef Jerky, 156–157
Garlic press, using, 16
Gluten-Free Puffy Snack Mix, 138
Granola, maple, *154–155*
Grass-fed, defined, 11
Great-Grandma's Spaghetti from Italy,
    110–112
Green beans, oven-roasted, *120–121*
Grilled Cheese, 114–115
Grocery shopping, 10–12
Guacamole, *148–149*

H

Healthy "Fruit Punch," 199
Homemade Hot Cocoa, 198
Honey-Mustard Chicken, 132

I

Ice pop mold and sticks, using, 16.
See also Snacks
Immersion blender, 15, 105
Ingredients. *See also specific
ingredients*
about: real food definition and, 10
buying, 10–12
Clean Fifteen, 11
Dirty Dozen vs., 10–11
grocery store label definitions
(organic, natural, grass-fed,
pasture raised, cage-free,
free-range), 11–12
measuring dry and liquid, 15–16
organic, 10–11
substitutions, 20–23
where to buy, 13

K

Kale Chips, 168
Katie. *See* Dessinger, Katie
Kid-Friendly Broccoli, 113
Kimball, Paul
about, 7–8
Berry Yogurt Ice Pops, 146
Black Bean Soup, 72–73
Blueberry-Banana Ice Pops, 144
Cheeseburger Soup, 106–107
Cheesy Beef, Potato, & Carrot
Casserole, 133–135
Creamed Cauliflower, 74–75
Egg Drop Soup, *76–77*
Egg Fried Rice, 78–79
Fall Smoothie, 197
Grilled Cheese, 114–115
Guacamole, *148–149*
Margherita Pizza, 85–*87*
Monkey Salad, 147
Pasta Salad, 65
Pineapple-Lemon Ice Pops, 145
Pinto Gallo (Gallo Pinto), 116–117
Pizza Cauliflower Soup, 104–105
Taco Cheese Sauce, *152–153*
Trail Mix, 139

Kitchen equipment, use and safety,
17–19. *See also specific recipes*
baking sheet (rimmed), 46
blenders, 14–15
dehydrator, 16, 154
food processor, 13
garlic press, 16
graters, 15
ice pop mold and sticks, 16
immersion blender, 15, 105
knives, 17–19
measuring cups and spoons, 15–16
oven, 14
peelers, 15
stovetop, 13–14
Knives, using safely, 17–19

L

Langford, Abigail
about, 8
Bacon-Wrapped Dates, 140–141
Baked Oatmeal Squares, *42–43*
Caramel Carrots, 101
Chia Pudding, *26–27*
Chicken Broth, 97
Chocolate Chip Cookies, 188–189
Crispy, Crunchy Potatoes, *118*–119
Cucumber Salad, 50–51
Easy, Cheesy Popcorn, 169
Flourless Banana Split Pancakes,
30–31
Fried Broccoli & Cauliflower, 96
Garden-Fresh Pesto Pasta,
108–109
Gluten-Free Puffy Snack Mix, 138
Lentil Soup, *56–57*
Oven-Baked Eggs & Bacon, 40
Oven Pancake, 41
Scrambled Eggs, 28–29
Lentils. *See* Beans and lentils
Lime-Marinated Steak, 126–127
Liquid ingredients, measuring, 16
Lunch, 49–93. *See also* Salads
Apple Sandwiches, *54–55*
Avocado Quesadilla, 66–67

Bacon Tomato Soup, 68–69
Baked Fish Sticks with Tartar
Sauce, 90–91
Best Burger with Secret Yum
Sauce, 92–93
Black Bean Soup, 72–73
BLTA Sandwich, 64
Cheeseburger Casserole, 80–81
Chicken Ranch Wraps with Greek
Yogurt Ranch Dressing, *88*–89
Creamed Cauliflower, 74–75
Easy Chicken Avocado Soup,
70–71
Egg Drop Soup, 76–77
Egg Fried Rice, 78–79
Lentil Soup, *56–57*
Mac 'n' Cheese, *58–59*
Margherita Pizza, 85–*87*
Taco Casserole, 82–83
Tomato, Zucchini, & Mozzarella
Bake, 84

M

Mac 'n' Cheese, *58–59*
Mango
Mango Lemonade, 192
Surf Smoothie, 193
Maple-Glazed Chicken Thighs, 98
Maple Granola, *154–155*
Margherita Pizza, 85–*87*
Mascarpone Cream, 32
Meal planning, 200–201
Measuring
cups and spoons for, 15–16
dry ingredients, 15–16
liquid ingredients, 16
Meat, buying, 11–12. *See also
specific meats*
Mediterranean Sun-Dried Tomato
Chicken, *130–131*
Mint, in Strawberry-Mint Smoothie,
196
Monkey Salad, 147
Muffins, "cornbread," *162–163*
Mug Brownies, *178–179*

N

Natural food, defined, 11
No-Bake Cookies, *174–175*
Nuts and seeds
    about: almond flour, 23; egg
        substitutes, 21, 22; nut/nut
        butter substitutes, 22
    Chia Pudding, *26–27*
    Maple Granola, *154–155*
    Monkey Salad, 147
    No-Bake Cookies, *174–175*
    Peanut Butter & Chocolate Mini
        Cups, 176
    Peanut Butter & Jelly Cups,
        172–173
    Strawberry–Chia Seed Jam,
        142–143
    Strawberry-Pecan Salad, *52–53*
    Trail Mix, 139

O

Oatmeal squares, baked, *42–43*
Organic food, 10–11
Oven-Baked Eggs & Bacon, 40
Oven-Baked Sweet Potato Fries,
    122–123
Oven Pancake, 41
Oven-Roasted Green Beans, *120–121*
Oven, using safely, 14

P

Pancakes
    Flourless Banana Split Pancakes,
        30–31
    Oven Pancake, 41
    School Day Blueberry Pancakes,
        34–35
Pasta
    Cheeseburger Casserole, 80–81
    Garden-Fresh Pesto Pasta,
        108–109
    Great-Grandma's Spaghetti from
        Italy, *110–112*
    Mac 'n' Cheese, *58–59*
    Pasta Salad, 65

Pasture raised, defined, 11
Paul. *See* Kimball, Paul
Peach Cobbler, 184–185
Peanut butter. *See* Nuts and seeds
Peelers, 15
Pineapple-Lemon Ice Pops, 145
Pizza Cauliflower Soup, 104–105
Pizza, margherita, 85–87
Planning meals, 200–201
Plantain Chips, 150
Popcorn, easy, cheesy, 169
Pork, buying, 11. *See also* Bacon;
    Sausage
Potatoes
    Cheesy Beef, Potato, & Carrot
        Casserole, 133–135
    Crispy, Crunchy Potatoes, *118*–119
    Simple Mashed Potatoes, 100
    Texas-Style Breakfast Tacos, 44
Pumpkin
    about: puree as egg substitute,
        21–22
    Fall Smoothie, 197
    Pumpkin Pie, 180–181

Q

Quesadilla, avocado, 66–67

R

Real food, defined, 10. *See also*
    Ingredients
Rice
    Egg Fried Rice, 78–79
    Gluten-Free Puffy Snack Mix, 138

S

Safety, in using equipment, 13–15,
    17–19
Salads
    Avocado Chicken Salad, 60–61
    Cucumber Salad, 50–51
    Monkey Salad, 147
    Pasta Salad, 65
    Strawberry Pecan Salad, *52–53*
    Taco Salad, 62–63

Sandwiches and wraps
    Apple Sandwiches, *54–55*
    Best Burger with Secret Yum
        Sauce, 92–93
    BLTA Sandwich, 64
    Breakfast Burritos, 36–37
    Chicken Ranch Wraps with Greek
        Yogurt Ranch Dressing, *88–89*
    Fish Tacos, 128–129
    Grilled Cheese, 114–115
    Texas-Style Breakfast Tacos, 44
Sauces. *See also* Pasta
    Greek Yogurt Ranch Dressing, 89
    Secret Yum Sauce, 93
    Super-Quick Gravy, 99
    Tartar Sauce, 91
Sausage
    Breakfast Burritos, 36–37
    Breakfast Casserole, 45
    Texas-Style Breakfast Tacos, 44
    Turkey Breakfast Sausage, *46–47*
Scrambled Eggs, 28–29
Secret Yum Sauce, 93
Simple Mashed Potatoes, 100
Smoothies. *See* Drinks
Snacks, 137–169. *See also* Bread
    about: using ice pop mold and
        sticks, 16
    Bacon-Wrapped Dates, 140–141
    Berry Yogurt Ice Pops, 146
    Blueberry-Banana Ice Pops, 144
    Buffalo Wings, 160–161
    Easy, Cheesy Popcorn, 169
    Garlic Beef Jerky, 156–157
    Gluten-Free Puffy Snack Mix, 138
    Guacamole, *148–149*
    Kale Chips, 168
    Monkey Salad, 147
    Pineapple-Lemon Ice Pops, 145
    Plantain Chips, 150
    Strawberry–Chia Seed Jam,
        142–143
    Taco Cheese Sauce, *152–153*
    Trail Mix, 139
    White Hot Chocolate, 151

Soups
    Bacon Tomato Soup, 68–69
    Black Bean Soup, 72–73
    Cheeseburger Soup, 106–107
    Chicken Broth, 97
    Easy Chicken Avocado Soup,
        70–71
    Egg Drop Soup, *76–77*
    Lentil Soup, *56–57*
    Pizza Cauliflower Soup, 104–105
    Turkey Chili, 102–103
Soy substitutes, 22
Spears, Anthony
    about, 8–9
    Baked Fish Sticks with Tartar
        Sauce, 90–91
    Best Burger with Secret Yum
        Sauce, 92–93
    Cheeseburger Casserole, 80–81
    Chicken Ranch Wraps with Greek
        Yogurt Ranch Dressing, 88–89
    Garlic Beef Jerky, 156–157
    Grandma's Overnight Breakfast
        Casserole, 45
    Great-Grandma's Spaghetti from
        Italy, *110–112*
    Homemade Hot Cocoa, 198
    Mango Lemonade, 192
    Maple-Glazed Chicken Thighs, 98
    Oven-Baked Sweet Potato Fries,
        122–123
    Oven-Roasted Green Beans,
        120–121

Peach Cobbler, 184–185
Pumpkin Pie, 180–181
Strawberry Cheesecake, 182–183
Strawberry-Pecan Salad, *52–53*
Super-Quick Gravy, 99
Taco Casserole, 82–83
Texas-Style Breakfast Tacos, 44
Tiramisu French Toast, 32–33
Starches, as thickening agents, 23
Stovetop, safe use of, 13–14
Strawberries. *See* Berries
Substitutions, 20–23
Super-Quick Gravy, 99
Surf Smoothie, 193
Sweet potato fries, oven-baked,
    122–123

T
Taco Casserole, 82–83
Taco Cheese Sauce, *152–153*
Tacos, 44, 128–129
Taco Salad, 62–63
Tapioca starch, 23
Tartar Sauce, 91
Texas-Style Breakfast Tacos, 44
Thickening agents, 23
Tiramisu French Toast, 32–33
Tomatoes
    Margherita Pizza, 85–87
    Mediterranean Sun-Dried
        Tomato Chicken, *130*–131
    sandwiches/wraps with. *See*
        Sandwiches and wraps

soups with. *See* Soups
Tomato, Zucchini, & Mozzarella
    Bake, 84
Trail Mix, 139
Turkey. *See also* Bacon; Sausage
    about: buying, 11–12
    Apple Sandwiches, *54–55*
    Great-Grandma's Spaghetti from
        Italy, *110–112*
    Turkey Breakfast Sausage, 46–47
    Turkey Chili, 102–103

V
Vegetables, buying, 10. *See also
    specific vegetables*

W
Week of family dinners, 200–201
Wheat flour substitutes, 23
White Hot Chocolate, 151
Will. *See* Bartlett, Will

Y
Yogurt
    Berry Yogurt Ice Pops, 146
    Greek Yogurt Ranch Dressing, 89
    Pineapple-Lemon Ice Pops, 145
    Surf Smoothie, 193

Z
Zucchini, in Tomato, Zucchini, &
    Mozzarella Bake, 84